WHA'
LAUGHING AT?

WHAT ARE YOU LAUGHING AT?

A comprehensive guide to the comedic event

DAN O'SHANNON

BLOOMSBURY

LONDON · NEW DELHI · NEW YORK · SYDNEY

Bloomsbury Academic

An imprint of Bloomsbury Publishing Plc

175 Fifth Avenue
New York
NY 10010
USA

50 Bedford Square
London
WC1B 3DP
UK

www.bloomsbury.com

First published in 2012 by the Continuum International Publishing Group Inc
Reprinted by Bloomsbury Academic 2013

Library of Congress Cataloging-in-Publication Data
A catalog record for this book is available from the Library of Congress.

ISBN: PB: 978-1-4411-629-39

Typeset by Fakenham Prepress Solutions, Fakenham, Norfolk NR21 8NN
Printed and bound in the United States of America

CONTENTS

Introduction ix

Overview 1

1   Common comedy theories 1
2   The comedic event 7
3   Documenting the comedic event 16

PART ONE Elements of context: the reception factors 21

1   The receiver and his world 23

1.1   The line between funny and not funny 23
1.2   A comedy frame of mind 25
1.3   The duality of comedy: two types of laughter 27
1.4   Early reception factors 32
1.5   Levels of social interaction 35

2   Elements of communication 43

2.1   Modes of communication 43
2.2   Device and specific device 49

3   Vehicles 55

3.1   Vehicles 55
3.2   Vehicle-based reception factors 77

4   Level of control and identifying the source 89

4.1   Level of control 89
4.2   Identifying the source 93

PART TWO Comedic Information 105

5 Fundamental components 107

    5.1 The receiver's brain: hard-wired for comedy? 107

    5.2 Comedic information: the triangle 108

    5.3 The core variables 114

6 Incongruity 121

    6.1 Incongruity 121

    6.2 Estimating levels of incongruity 133

    6.3 Types of incongruity 145

7 Cognitive process 155

    7.1 Cognitive process: overview 155

    7.2 Level one: straightforward information 158

    7.3 Level two: gap-filling 176

    7.4 Level three: recontextualization 184

8 Variations 202

    8.1 Exploring the four corners of the triangle 202

    8.2 What are practical jokes? 209

9 Comedy and entropy 211

    9.1 Sustaining the laugh 211

    9.2 Entropy 222

PART THREE Enhancers, inhibitors, and aspects of awareness 237

10 How comedic information triggers enhancers and inhibitors 239

    10.1 Overview 239

    10.2 On-going social needs: superiority, identification, and inclusion 242

    10.3 Aspects of awareness 247

11 Elements of the joke's communication, structure, and content 260

    11.1 Resuming the chart: the joke as a whole 260
    11.2 Elements of communication and structure 261
    11.3 Elements of content 267
    11.4 The target 273

Summing it all up 283
    The completed chart 283
    Final thoughts and acknowledgments 289
Index 293

INTRODUCTION

If you're looking for a book that will teach you how to write comedy, I suggest you keep moving. You still have time to pick up a copy of *Writing Big Yucks for Big Bucks* before the store closes. However, if you want to understand the bigger picture—what is comedy, why do we respond to it in the way we do—then you've come to the right place.

* * *

I've always been what you might call a comedy detective. I observe and create comedy and I study the laugh. That's the true mission of the comedy detective: understand the laugh. What's really going on? What invisible factors are shaping the response?

The answers haven't always come easily. In one instance a single laugh became a 15-year riddle.

I heard it on March 12, 1977. I was barely 15 years old, living in rural Ohio. It was a Saturday night, and like most of America, my family was watching *The Mary Tyler Moore Show*. The episode, called "Lou Dates Mary," chronicles an awkward date between Mary Richards and her boss, Lou Grant. The show builds to a moment on Mary's couch, where the two characters slowly go in for a kiss—only to start laughing as they realize how silly it is for them to try to turn their relationship into something it's not.

The climactic moment felt slightly off to me. But it wasn't the scene. The actors were brilliant and the situation was genuinely funny. It was the studio audience. The laugh started out loud and full, but there was an odd quick taper to it. The moment left me hanging somehow.

I didn't think about it again until years later, when I was writing and producing *Cheers*. (Coincidentally, one of the writers on the staff was David Lloyd, who wrote many episodes of *The Mary Tyler Moore Show*, including "Lou Dates Mary.") We were filming an episode in which the less-than-ambitious Norm does a joke where he starts to talk about taking his career and marriage seriously, but he's only kidding and can't even complete the sentence without cracking himself up. At this I heard a familiar response from the studio audience: a shriek of laughter followed by a too-quick taper. And suddenly I had the answer. I now understood the laugh I'd heard 15 years earlier.

(The explanation is in Chapter 4, p. 58.)

* * *

The first step toward understanding the laugh is to understand what comedy is and how it works. Unfortunately, there's one tiny problem:

Nobody agrees on what comedy is or how it works.

For centuries, theorists have argued over comedy's unifying link. Incongruity, superiority, aggression, surprise, and relief keep popping up, either singly or in combinations. I've seen the amateur expert analyze the linguistic structure of a few jokes and extrapolate their conclusions to account for all of comedy. The true amateurs, meanwhile, divide comedy into various "forms" (satire, farce, insult humor, wordplay, gross-out humor, etc.) and proceed from there, not knowing that they've already lost the battle.

And so we come to the purpose of this book: the creation of a new and comprehensive model of comedy; a model upon which any joke or humorous incident (along with the reaction it gets) can be examined effectively.

This model will allow for any variation in comedy's arsenal; linguistic jokes as well as slapstick, intentional comedy along with unintentional. It accounts for the decay of old jokes, the nature of practical jokes, and the existence of meta-comedy. It will also catalog the variables of transmission that are so crucial to comedy response.

I'll be presenting new ideas in this book, as well as rearranging some old ones. By the end, you'll have a true understanding of what happens when man meets comedy. You'll see how every comedic experience is unique, and you'll understand the possible factors that go into every laugh.

Think of it as *The Comedy Detective's Handbook*.

Who am I and why should you listen to me?

Before plunging into a book of this size, you may want to know why you should trust me. Fair enough.

For me, the road began in 1970. I was sitting on a gymnasium floor with the rest of my class for a school assembly. There was a man on stage and he was making us laugh. I have no idea what he was doing; in fact, I have no recollection of the day at all except for the moment when the man paused. He was waiting for us to catch our collective breath, and he leaned against the microphone stand and mused, "There's nothing like the feeling of making people laugh."

The click inside of me was deafening. I remember looking around the room to see if anyone else had heard what I heard; or rather, connected with it like I did. Amazingly, the remark had passed over them. But they were changed, because in that moment I saw them as people, but maybe they could also be … audience. I was eight years old, and I'd found my calling.

I was going to be funny.

Thus began the loneliest period of my life. I was full of enthusiasm but didn't have the slightest clue how to be funny. I just knew what made me laugh. Back then it was Jerry Lewis, so I became Jerry Lewis. I learned quickly and painfully that there is also nothing like the feeling of not making people laugh. I was too young to understand the enormous difference between a character doing comedy in the context of a made-up movie and someone enacting the same behavior in real life.

In my teens I was studying sitcoms on TV, recognizing joke patterns. I analyzed cartoons. In the library I found and devoured James Thurber and

Robert Benchley, trying hard to duplicate their styles in my writing. The problem? I had no perspective, no point of view. I was simply too young to generate credible material. And let's remember: my audience was mostly other kids—not exactly the kindest crowd.

Unencumbered by popularity, I began to discover books about comedy. The first one I ever read was Steve Allen's *The Funny Men*, written in 1956. A revelation. Around this time Leonard Maltin was writing about cartoons, comedy teams, *The Little Rascals* ... everything I watched on TV that no one wanted to discuss with me on any real critical level. I read books by Joe Adamson, George Burns, Milt Josefsberg, Walter Kerr, everything I could lay my hands on.

At age 19 I started doing stand-up comedy with original material. And I found out that indeed, there is nothing like the feeling of making people laugh.

This book is the result of what I learned over the next 30 years.

(Are you still reading this in a bookstore? Are you trying to decide between this book and *Being Funny for Money* by that guy who wrote for *My Little Margie*? Did you flip ahead and see all the diagrams I have?)

You'll notice that there's almost no citing of other comedy research in these pages. The contents are based on my observations, first as a stand-up comic and then as a sitcom writer and producer. Fortunately, I was able to work on some of the best shows in television: *Newhart*, *Cheers*, *Frasier*, *Modern Family*, and many more. I worked alongside brilliant writers, actors, and directors, and I kept my eyes and ears open the whole time.

I've written thousands of jokes and attended thousands of rehearsals. I've taken part in endless rewrites, all in the service of making scripts funnier. The stage has been my laboratory, and I've witnessed the reactions of hundreds of thousands of people to joke after joke after joke, every variation imaginable. I learned that we can use jokes to trigger every feeling in the psyche. It got to the point where I could hear when the laugh was off; I could hear when we got the right response but for the wrong reason. I learned the language of laughter, not by reading about it in a book, but by immersion. I lived there.

Before embarking . . .

If you're going to plow ahead, there is one rule:

Lose your comedy prejudice.

There are readers who will go into this book with preconceptions. Some believe that All Comedy is About Truth or that The Job of Comedy is to Provoke. I would urge you to not confuse your preferred use of comedy with the definition of comedy itself. Comedy is flexible. It can be a sword, it can be a Band-Aid. It can make us think, it can distract us from thinking.

Also:

We all have individual senses of humor. This means that there will naturally be comedic examples in here that you do not find funny. Some are old-fashioned, others may just not do it for you. This does not diminish their value as examples. They have all been found funny by individuals or audiences at some point, and that's enough.

The study of comedy is not limited to that which is currently popular, critically embraced, or personally favored. We'll pull comedy from silent films to *South Park*, from people getting hit in the groin in home videos to mash-ups on YouTube.

And for an eight-year-old I used to know, we'll even find a little Jerry Lewis.

Overview

1 COMMON COMEDY THEORIES

Comedy appears to be a shape-shifter. It comes at us in so many ways and attaches itself to so many emotions that it's difficult to pin the thing down to a single, workable model. Is it really possible for the humor of Mark Twain to be related to the sight of the Three Stooges slapping each other senseless? A collection of Calvin and Hobbes can elicit laughs. So can a man falling downstairs, or a co-worker doing an impression of the boss, or a toddler swearing, or a joke that's so unfunny it becomes hilarious, or an outlandish drawing of genitalia, or a song parody, or *His Girl Friday*, or a dog trying to eat peanut butter, or the fact that some people still use the word "outlandish."

So what is the unifying link? There are several well-known theories as to just what comedy is. Since many of these come up routinely in comedy discussion, and because you don't want to look like an idiot if you get trapped in one of these conversations, here is a brief rundown of the more familiar schools of thought. But I'm not going into a lot of detail—what am I, Wikipedia?

Comedy is pain

"When I fall down, it's tragedy. When you fall down, it's comedy." This is the old adage that describes pain theory. We get to laugh at the misfortune of others from a safe distance, say, a theater seat or across the street.

Time can also be the safe distance that allows us to laugh at pain. From the comfortable seat of adulthood we can laugh at the gut-wrenching emotional pain we suffered as children and teenagers.

There's another old saying: "Tragedy plus time equals comedy." Few people would think to make a joke about the sinking of the Titanic in April 1912. The tragedy needed to be a safe distance away, the victims less real. (As a side note, our society has, over the years, shortened the time between a tragic event and the inevitable jokes. There are two reasons for this. First, there seems to be a race to get the first joke out, as though a tragedy is now a challenge to see who can cause the most shock. Second, our technology enables everyone to have a national spotlight. Even if people made a Titanic joke in 1912, no national outlet would ever think of printing it, so those jokes never registered on the public radar.)

The value of the safe distance allows us to enjoy pain on several levels. If we see Moe smack Curly with a tire iron, distance allows us to absorb the shock of the blow vicariously. We can identify with Curly; we can be shocked by the violence, all without feeling the pain. There may also be an unconscious element of relief in the laughter, in the sudden realization that we can be close to this experience and not be hurt.

Or maybe we identify with Moe, which leads nicely into ...

Cruelty/aggression

This school of thought states that we can enjoy aggression toward others safely through comedy. We sublimate aggression in real life, and seeing it happen safely can be a release. This would contribute to the popularity of insult humor. But then, so does ...

Superiority

There are those who believe that all comedy creates feelings of superiority. Seeing someone painted as a buffoon can cause us to feel a sudden jolt of elevation in our own status, which is then expressed as laughter.

Identification

Identification is recognition of our own traits, history, or emotions in the comedy. Identification is the bread and butter of observational humorists who go on and on about relationships and the differences between men and women. Since the audience is generally made up of men and/or women, this kind of humor is very relatable.

Subversion

This is laughter at the inappropriate. We may find great joy in railing against authority through comedy, or enjoy comedy that pushes the boundaries of social acceptability. We may be shocked into laughter or enjoy comedy that we also find off-putting. Dark humor may be included here. Perpetrators of this type of comedy are surrogates for the sides of ourselves we know we shouldn't express. When we see our sublimated feelings or desires expressed, we may also feel ...

Relief

Freud believed that laughter is the result of a release of tension. This can be the dramatic tension built up within the joke or within the narrative surrounding the joke (as in the comedy relief that pops up in a dramatic situation). It can also refer to a release of social tension, such as when we break the ice with humor or use comedy to approach subjects and behaviors that are uncomfortable to bring up. The relief caused by the use of humor is a release of tension.

Irony

Irony is often confused with coincidence. While sheer coincidence is random, irony is based on goals. For example, if a character (or a society) needs to accomplish a specific goal, an ironic twist may determine that it is achieved in an unexpected way, or that the goal is achieved but produces the opposite of the intended effect. It may also be that what the character really wanted all along can only happen when the stated goal fails. Take all those old pulp fiction stories in which an obsessed character finally gets everything he wanted … forever … because he's actually in Hell! Now there's some irony for you.

Here are two examples of coincidence, only one of which results in irony:

1 I have a daughter, named Chloe, from my first marriage. After my divorce I married a woman who has a daughter named Chloe. Friends have called this ironic, but it's only a coincidence.

2 When I was in my twenties I decided to see a therapist (never mind why). I didn't have much money, so I went to a low-budget counseling center where I could be interviewed and then assigned to a therapist based on my problems and goals. I asked for a female therapist, because I didn't want to feel like I was talking to my father, who was the source of some of my problems. They assigned me to a young lady named Terry—which is my father's name. This is more irony than coincidence, since I was now using a Terry to try to overcome the effects of another Terry.

It's coincidental, rather than ironic, that both stories have to do with the duplication of names.

In comedy, there are two kinds of irony:

1   Irony within the narrative: in this case, all the pieces that create irony
    exist within the story being told. O. Henry wrote stories with ironic
    twists and endings.

2   Ironic laughter, or ironic comedy: here, the irony does not exist within
    the dramatic structure. If we hear a joke so awful that we laugh at
    how bad it is, we are taking part in the irony; in other words, the joke
    did not contain irony; irony was provided by our response. Why is it
    ironic? Because the intent of the joke was to get laughter, and it did—
    but for the wrong reason.

Disappointment

In the broadest sense, disappointment theory is based on the premise that we
laugh at the unexpected. Some have referred to this as thwarting of expectation. In many jokes, a set-up leads us one way, and the punchline takes us
in an unexpected direction. A man is walking across the street. Suddenly, and
without warning, he drops into an open manhole. The surprise short-circuits
us in some way, shocking us into laughter.

Incongruity

Incongruity is the joining together of two or more disparate ideas for
humorous effect. This may be as basic as a photo of a man with a baby's head
superimposed over his own, or the old commercial in which a man sings in a
beautiful operatic voice about his lack of Rice Krispies. The brilliant silliness
of *Monty Python's Flying Circus* mines incongruity over and over with dazzling
effect—listing examples would fill up this book. One of my personal favorites:
the gathering of Karl Marx, Vladimir Lenin, Che Guevara, and Mao Zedong
into a panel where they are asked questions, not about communism, but about
sports and pop music for prizes.

Parts in search of an elephant

There is an old story about a group of blind men who touch an elephant to learn what it is like. One who touches the tusk concludes that elephants are like pipes. Another, touching the tail, believes that elephants are shaped like ropes. The man who puts his hands on the side of the animal announces that the creature is like a wall.

When we gather these basic theories together, it begins to look as though people have been approaching comedy from different directions. Some theories concern the comedy's content, others are based on the feelings that arise from the comedic experience, and others are process-related.

The problem is this: Every one of these theories can account for the primary cause of laughter in thousands of jokes. Therefore, they would seem to be canceling each other out as candidates for the "root of all comedy."

We need to step back and see these ideas as components of a larger, more comprehensive model.

For now, file these theories in the back of your head. You'll see them all again.

We're going to build an elephant.

WARNING: BEWARE THE BAD LISTS

A common approach to defining comedy is to start by breaking it into categories, then distracting everybody by defining the categories. If you Google "forms of comedy" you will find a number of charts and lists, some made by serious students of comedy, others by casual observers. Often, these lists seem thrown together with no clear parameters: one entry may be based on linguistic structure, while another is based on the effect it has on the audience. Still others are based on content. The result is that we have awkward stews of qualities and styles blended together and served up like so:

Types of comedy

Farce
Slapstick
Wordplay
Parody
Satire
Drawing-room comedy
Shock/gross-out humor
Insult humor

This list is virtually useless. How, for example, is one to categorize a gross insult that relies on wordplay occurring in a farce?

2 THE COMEDIC EVENT

Based on what we observe in our daily lives, we can easily surmise that an encounter with comedy goes something like this:

1 A receiver (this can be anyone—you, me, Mr. Stec next door) comes into contact with …

2 comedic information (a joke or any comedic stimulus), and has a …

3 response (laughter, a smile, the rolling of eyes, whatever).

Graphically, we may depict the incident as in (Figure a):

RECEIVER ⟶   ⟶ RESPONSE
**COMEDIC
INFORMATION**

Comedic information refers to anything we find funny, whether it's a formally structured joke or witnessing an amusing occurrence, or even the random funny thought. In this book, comedic information is represented by a triangle.

Using this diagram as a starting point, we can plug in any joke and note the response. And here's a joke now:

Did you hear about the Polish airline disaster? A two-seat Cessna crashed into a cemetery. So far they've recovered over 300 bodies.

You, the reader, may have had a response, but I don't know what it was (Figure b):

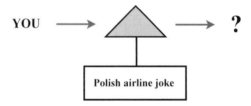

So I've called my Aunt Rita and told her the joke. This was her response (Figure c):

Perhaps Mike from next door will react differently (Figure d):

In these examples the joke is the only consistent element. Therefore, one might assume that different responses must be due to individual tastes. You, Aunt Rita, and Mike may simply have dissimilar senses of humor.

The truth, however, is more complicated. The receiver's journey through a joke is loaded with variables, any one of which can greatly alter the response. Without knowledge of these variables and how they work, the comedy detective simply flails around in the dark.

Expanding our view: The comedic event

First, we must accept that comedy is an experience. A joke written on a piece of paper is not comedy, any more than a stick of dynamite is an explosion. At best, information by itself can only be intended comedy. In order for it to work, it has to be activated by the receiver.

Let's go back to the Polish airline joke. You came across the words in a book written by a stranger who was not present to influence your response. On the other hand, Aunt Rita heard the joke from someone she loves, who was on the phone waiting for a reaction. You both encountered identical comedic information, but took part in very different comedic experiences.

This is why a good comedy detective doesn't attribute the laugh solely to the comedic information. He attributes it to the comedic event.

Using the above diagrams as a simple representation of the comedic event, our next step is to zoom in and take a closer look—particularly at those arrows, because it's within those arrows that so many variables come into play.

So let's chart the receiver's journey.

Part One: Elements of context (reception factors)

These are the elements of the joke's context, the pre-joke conditions that can affect our level of readiness to take in and appreciate comedy. Here are a few examples:

1   A great joke told by your best friend may provoke a different response from you than the same joke told by someone you despise.

2   If you're watching a movie in a crowded theater, you may be more likely to laugh than if you're watching it by yourself.

3   If you're drunk, any comedy may be extra funny or not funny at all.

4   A joke on a sitcom may annoy you, while the same joke in a play may earn your applause.

Some basic reception factors are shown in their place on the model (Figure e):

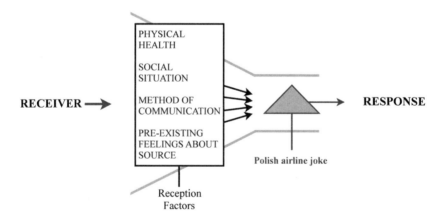

Part Two: Completion of the incongruous picture

Here we get to the triangle that represents the joke.

Back when you read about the Polish airline you took in the information, which made you fill in logical gaps to figure out that people were digging up bodies from a cemetery. Once the idea was assembled, you were free to enjoy (or not) the incongruities in the completed image (Figure f):

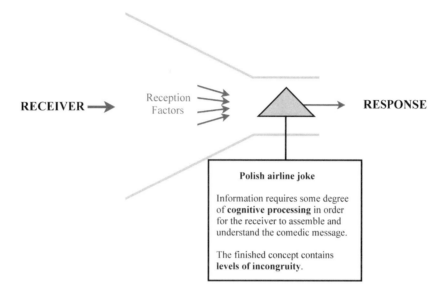

RECEIVER → Reception Factors → **RESPONSE**

Polish airline joke

Information requires some degree of **cognitive processing** in order for the receiver to assemble and understand the comedic message.

The finished concept contains **levels of incongruity**.

All comedic information has two core variables:

1 The amount of cognitive work it takes to assemble the incongruous concept.

2 The level of incongruity contained in the completed image.

Notice I'm saying "amount" and "level." Not all incongruity is equal, and not all comedic information requires the same amount of work to assemble or decode. Later on we'll discuss ways to estimate these levels, and see that their interaction has a significant effect on the nature of the receiver's response.

Don't be misled. While incongruity is a component in all comedy, not all comedy is incongruity. That would be like stating that tires are an element of all cars; therefore all cars are tires.

While we often laugh at high incongruity, it can also be overshadowed by other factors, such as when a joke triggers strong feelings of superiority or shock. These feelings can be so powerful that their impact dominates the experience in our minds—we're barely aware of the incongruity.

In addition, note that the level of incongruity in comedic information may be exceedingly low, to the point at which it is not a primary factor in the response. There is much to explain in this department, and we'll get to it all in Part Two.

[*Note for any ringers out there*: You may suspect that I'm heading in the direction of incongruity resolution theory, but rest assured: I'm not. As will be discussed in Chapter 6, incongruity resolution is based on flawed principles—I'll even go so far as to say that it's one of the biggest road-blocks to understanding comedy ever created.]

Part Three: Enhancers/inhibitors and aspects of awareness

Now that the brain has worked out the joke, the finished thought can trigger emotions in the receiver. These emotions can either enhance or inhibit the receiver's response to the incongruous picture (Figure g):

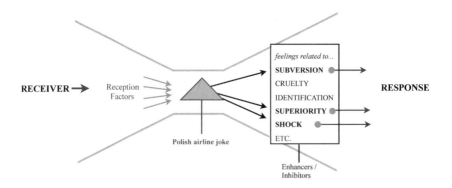

You'll recognize some of these feelings as being core components in those standard comedy theories from a few pages ago. In this model, they are triggered by recognition of the comedic idea.

A receiver hearing the Polish airline joke may have a response that is enhanced by the subversive nature of using a fatal plane crash as comedy.

He may also enjoy feelings of superiority over the protagonists, as well as the shock value. Another receiver's response may be inhibited owing to the morbid nature of the material or indignation at the slight on the Polish. As I write this, there has recently been an actual plane crash in a cemetery in Montana—talk about an inhibitor.

Examples of enhancer/inhibitors:

1   A receiver's reaction to foul language can enhance or inhibit his response to a joke.

2   A joke may cause an audience member to change his feelings for, or gain insight into, the character or person who delivered it. This may enhance or inhibit the response.

3   If the joke is about, say, a political figure or celebrity or family member, the joke will be enhanced or inhibited by the audience's feelings for that target.

4   Someone hearing an inside joke may have his or her appreciation enhanced simply by being aware that only a few people get it.

5   A receiver's appreciation for the execution of the joke may enhance the response.

Remember the old joke "Your mama's so fat she has her own ZIP code?" Once we figure it out, we're left with the image of a woman as large as a city. This is an impossible image—a highly incongruous one—and the enjoyment may be enhanced by the fact that it has some cruelty in it. Cruelty is an enhancer; it is not the joke. If someone simply says, "Your mama's very fat," we have cruelty but no discernible incongruity to make it comedically viable.

And of course, this very cruelty can be an inhibitor. If we have struggled with weight all our lives, we may not enjoy the incongruous picture of a woman as large as a city.

Reception factors vs. enhancers/inhibitors

The kid in the back of the room has a question. He wants to know if reception factors are the same as enhancers and inhibitors. Good question, kid in the back.

Reception factors are contextual variables, and indeed they trigger emotions that enhance or inhibit the experience, but their effect is at work before the joke can make an impact. We may call them pre-joke enhancers/inhibitors if we wish, but we note them separately, for two reasons:

1 To reinforce the idea that these factors are in play before the joke, giving us a state of mind prior to contact with the comedic information. Reception factors set the stage for the joke, which is different than reaction to the joke itself.

2 The way reception factors trigger feelings is fairly straightforward, as we'll see. However, once we've encountered the joke, all hell breaks loose. We are cognizant of the joke in multiple aspects of awareness.

Aspects of awareness

We not only experience the joke, we experience *the experience* of the joke. We do this in multiple aspects of awareness, any of which may trigger an array of feelings.

We are aware of the joke's internal reality (a man walking into a bar, a sitcom scene, whatever), while we are simultaneously aware of the joke's existence in our own reality. We have a critical appreciation of the joke and its execution. We may even have a response that is shaped by our awareness of other receivers' responses. Any strong feeling in any of these aspects of awareness can make or break the experience.

With this last set of variables in place, our simple diagram of the comedic event now looks like this (Figure h):

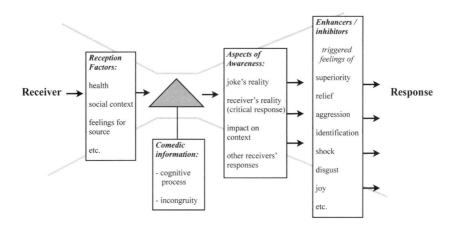

A more fluid approach

By understanding the nature of the comedic event, we don't tangle ourselves up in the "all comedy is this" and "all comedy is that" debate. Any enhancer or inhibitor triggered by any element of the comedic event may be the dominant factor in the receiver's response. In other words, there's room for everybody.

To illustrate the point, let's resurrect comedy detective Arthur Schopenhauer, who, like many others, believed that all comedy is incongruity. Schopenhauer went so far as to say that the more incongruous a concept, the more explosive the laugh. This is simply not true.

The lower the incongruity of a joke, the more it resembles reality, and thus the more we can relate to it. Identification is a strong enhancer. This is why some people laugh more at the soft comedy of *The Andy Griffith Show* than at the high incongruity of *Monty Python's Flying Circus*.

(I should point out that *Monty Python*'s comedy, as highly incongruous as it could be, was often enhanced by subversiveness, and shock, as it poked fun at many sacred cows.)

Throughout this book, we'll see many examples of low incongruity humor that triggers strong enhancers. These enhancers provide the necessary wattage for low incongruity to succeed.

Notice that Schopenhauer also does not take into account any contextual variables, such as the receiver's feelings for the source of the comedy, or even whether or not the receiver is having a bad day. He is trying to create a direct correlation using only the joke and the laugh. This only works if:

1 Every joke is floating in space with no context.

2 Every receiver has the same comedic preferences.

Oh, Schopenhauer!

This is, of course, a simple overview. In the chapters which follow, we will explore every variable, seeing how each can affect response. We'll also take apart that mysterious triangle and learn how our brains interact with comedic information.

3 DOCUMENTING THE COMEDIC EVENT

The rest of this book will be laid out in an order that approximates the receiver's journey through a comedic event. This breaks down into three parts:

1 Reception factors. We will list and discuss elements of context and how they influence the receiver.

2 Comedic information (the incongruous picture). This is hardcore stuff: how jokes work. These are the elements of structure and content. We'll also discuss comedic entropy.

3 Enhancers/inhibitors. This covers the way in which elements from the joke trigger feelings that effect the laugh. This includes the various aspects of awareness.

While everything is laid out systematically, there is no law that says you have to read it in order (I checked). Hardcore comedy enthusiasts may wish to leap straight to Part Two and read about how jokes work. Part Two is full of all kinds of goodies for people who study this sort of thing, so be my guest.

Creating a comedy diagnostic

Let's say you want to know why a certain joke got the response it did from a single receiver or from multiple receivers. Or perhaps you heard a laugh that was way out of proportion to the joke being told, and being a good comedy detective your curiosity is stirred.

How do we examine the event? How can we haul it up on the rack and take a good look at it?

Naturally, you would want to have as much information about the event as possible. That's where our handy checklist comes in. We're going to build it as we make our way through the book. It will contain every important variable in comedy, and with it, we can record the details of any comedic event and theorize as to the likely primary factors motivating the response.

Think of it as documenting the scene of a crime.

This list will be in the form of a chart as seen here:

	ELEMENTS OF COMEDIC EVENT	INFLUENCE ON RECEIVER
VARIABLE		
VARIABLE		
VARIABLE		
VARIABLE		

Someday, a chart such as this may serve as the basis for a working comedy diagnostic—a standardized data-gathering tool for noting comedy response. Amassed on a large scale (millions of jokes, millions of receivers), these data would give us a virtual topography of humor preferences in this country. We could track preferences by age, ethnicity, socio-economic status, geographic region. We could chart comedic evolution over time, as well as identify regional migrations in mass comedy preferences. Eventually, one could even create a test for measuring senses of humor based on national averages.

But we're getting ahead of ourselves. The focus of this book is to familiarize you with comedy, rather than to provide any method for data gathering. Therefore, we'll concentrate primarily on the left side of the chart—elements of comedic event—and not worry about filling out the right side—influence on the receiver. We will discuss ways in which each variable can affect a receiver, but that's as far as we'll go.

[*Note*: Don't drive yourself crazy splitting hairs and trying to get the charts perfect. Their use in this book is primarily for idea reinforcement; to get you used to thinking in terms of these variables. You are not expected to actually carry a chart around with you.]

By merely understanding the nature of the variables, you will be equipped with enough information to give you probable answers as you learn the language of the laugh.

Expanding the definition of "joke"

To make things easier, the word "joke" will be taken to mean *any* comedic information, whether it is a self-contained language-based structure, or a bit of physical business, or an amusing thing you saw out of your window the other day, or a toddler pronouncing words in a funny way.

Those who study jokes may find themselves uncomfortable with the idea that a dog trying bite a flashlight beam is a "joke" because it isn't self-contained comedy; no set-up has been provided to make the punchline clear. As we'll see, we can always find the set-up and we can always find the punchline. We just have to know where to look.

"Laugh" vs. "response"

I tend to use these terms somewhat interchangeably, but I should be clear on this. A successful joke need not necessarily elicit a physical laugh—I've often heard people respond to comedic information with a nod and a muttered "that's funny." A lack of laughter does not mean failure as comedy. And, as we'll learn, laughter can also exist for reasons that have little to do with how funny the information is to the receiver.

PART ONE

ELEMENTS OF CONTEXT: THE RECEPTION FACTORS

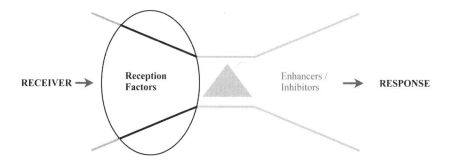

In this section we map out the elements of comedy's context and learn how they can affect the way we experience comedy.

1

The receiver and his world

1.1 THE LINE BETWEEN FUNNY AND NOT FUNNY

Let's start with the big question. What makes something funny? Of all the data that flows into our minds every day, why does some of it make us laugh?

This question has sent many people scurrying to study the information itself. Surely "funny information" must be different than "unfunny information," right? Is there a certain magical structure that defines it as comedy? A universal element of content?

We can dig through a mountain of material looking for that elusive demarcation, but if we restrict the search solely to information, our conclusions will be insufficient. There is simply no joke or joke-type that always works, nor one that accounts for every laugh or successful comedic event. This is not merely a case of people having individual senses of humor.

Structure, or pattern recognition, is not the answer—for every standard joke structure, we can just as easily communicate a ton of ideas using the same rules without creating comedy. This is why it's so easy to deconstruct jokes, but so hard to successfully reverse engineer comedy out of the disassembled pieces.

So what is the line between that which is funny and that which is not?

You can have what you believe to be a foolproof joke, but execute it badly and the receiver will not find it funny. Tell it on an off-day for the receiver, or have it told by someone whom the receiver hates. The receiver may be unable or unwilling to see the material as funny. In other circumstances, your joke may have been a tremendous success.

The target, it seems, is always moving. And so there is our line: an ever-moving perception in the mind of the receiver.

Thus we alter the question. Instead of asking what makes some information funny, we ask: What is it that determines whether or not a receiver experiences information as funny?

And here's where it gets fun: *the experience of information as "funny" is a choice made by the receiver.*

In 1981, Professor Marvin Minsky wrote the following, in his paper "Jokes and Their Relation to the Cognitive Unconscious":

> When you tell a young child "I am telling a lie" then, if he is old enough to reason so, he will think: 'If that is false, then he's not telling a lie. But then, so it must be true. But then, it must be a lie for it says so. But then—". And so on, back and forth.
>
> … Often, the listener first seems puzzled, then troubled, then finally laughs. "That's funny," he says. "Tell me another liar joke."

We can practically see the tumblers in the child's head as he tries to figure out where to fit the paradox in his mind. Finally, it gets chalked up to, literally, non-sense. It's supposed to make the head spin in this delightfully unproductive way.

There is also recognition of play. Your words tricked the child into looking for something that wasn't there; it's a game. This is important: if a child is intimidated into trying to solve a paradox out of fear or the threat of shame, then play is not recognized, and the information will not be registered as a "joke." A far less pleasing anxiety will manifest. Play must be recognized here.

The child *chooses* to see the information as funny.

Getting the receiver to make the choice

If we wish to make an audience laugh, be it an audience of one or millions, we need them to make the decision that the information we give them is funny. The audience must choose over and over, instantly co-creating and maintaining alternate realities, experiencing rippling "what if's." We persuade them every way we can, taking short cuts with pattern recognition, with our performance, by maximizing enhancers, dialing down inhibitors. It's not enough to tell the joke. You gotta sell the joke.

At the end of the day the receiver is the goalie, the final arbiter of what gets in and what doesn't.

Our job is to understand the variables that influence the receiver's decision. It helps to understand our relationship to comedy.

1.2 A COMEDY FRAME OF MIND

Recognizing comedic potential: two triggers

In order to experience comedic information as "funny," the receiver first needs to recognize that the information has (or has had) the potential to be funny. In other words, the brain needs to know that it can file the data under comedy. This is not a labored process; it may take microseconds. Whether or not it is then enjoyed is a different matter.

There are two ways to alert the receiver that information can be experienced as humorous. Without either or both of these core triggers, comedy does not exist.

One trigger is the identification of safe incongruity. We'll spend many delightful hours examining incongruity later on. For now, we will simply say that the recognition of incongruity that is safe (or harmless, or benign, pick a synonym) is a visceral trigger, one that can even startle us into laughter.

Interestingly, this can also happen with information that is unsafe, like the news of a great tragedy. The mind can find the information so shocking or threatening that it rejects the truth of it, rendering the information nonsense. The brain then tries to make sense of the nonsense by filing it under comedy – just as Minsky's kid when faced with a paradox. Perhaps you've burst out laughing at bad news or seen someone else to do it.

The other core trigger is the cognitive/social trigger. This may be the recognition of play or humorous intent. It may be a conscious decision to look at events with an eye toward comedic potential. We alert each other to comedic potential all the time. An example might be as simple as starting an exchange with "Here's a joke." Often, jokes start with standard phrasing, such as, "A guy walks into a bar" or "What do you call a blank when it blanks?" or "Knock knock." The invoking of standard phrases cues the receiver, whose brain is now on the watch for possible comedic connections.

In other situations, comedy is more broadly announced—if we're watching a sitcom we know there should be jokes ahead.

But what if there is no announcement, no standard wording? What if you're in a restaurant and your friend says something sarcastic or inappropriate on the spur of the moment?

The source of the humor—in this case your friend—has probably found other ways to tip you off, whether by leaning in and speaking in a way that tells you his words are not for public consumption, or with his expression, or the way he delivers the line.

Perhaps you've experienced hearing jokes from someone with a dry delivery. This involves the withholding of obvious cues, so the humor slips out more unexpectedly. Occasionally, the delivery is too dry and the joke flies by unnoticed. The problem isn't that you didn't get the joke—you didn't even know you were supposed to be looking for one. Dick Cavett has told a story of the first time he did stand-up comedy. He asked the management to introduce him as "a man who wants to talk to you." He bombed, simply because the audience did not know that comedy was on the table. By the time they realized it, perhaps it was too late.

EVOLUTION OF THE EMOTICON

In the old days, when people wrote letters to each other on paper, they would occasionally write "ha ha" after a joke, to make sure the recipient knew the writer was being funny. When email took over the world in the 1980s, there were millions of instances of people writing jokes in their mail and the recipient being hurt or offended, not realizing that a joke had been made. Without standard verbal and visual cues, people had trouble consistently recognizing comedy as comedy. Thus the smiley face started appearing after any line that was meant to be a joke. This was joined by the winking face and a host of other expressions designed to give the reader a sense of the attitude beneath the words.

With "found" humor—those funny things we notice on our own—something out of the ordinary draws attention to itself and we see the comedy in it, even if we do so retroactively. Certainly, when we're in the right frame of mind we'll notice some pretty subtle connections. But with all that's going on inside our craniums, there are dozens of possible humorous connections that pass us by every day because we're not looking for them.

1.3 THE DUALITY OF COMEDY: TWO TYPES OF LAUGHTER

Our two triggers for identifying comedic potential hint at a much larger dichotomy.

The vast landscape of what we call comedy is actually a blending of two types of recognition: visceral and social. We have joined and overlapped these two recognitions so seamlessly over the centuries that we do not see them as separate ingredients. It does not help the confusion that we respond to both with the same sound.

Laughter is both a natural response and a social display. Often, it is more of one than the other, which means we cannot judge the funniness of a joke simply by the laugh.

Laughter as a visceral response

As human beings, we constantly measure incoming data against our own storehouse of mental probabilities. We do it automatically, our attention immediately grabbed by incongruity. This may be a feature of self-preservation. When we were vulnerable, primitive creatures, we must have known that anything beyond our comfort zone could pose a threat to survival.

Imagine us as simpler beings, wired to be on the alert for incongruity because anything out of the ordinary might kill us. When incongruity is recognized—a shadow at the wrong time, an unfamiliar noise in the jungle— all our red flags go up, our hackles are raised, our bodies are flooded with adrenaline, and our pulses pound. Fear and/or aggression surge as we prepare to fight, flee, or die. And then the incongruity turns out to be harmless.

Suddenly, all the switches are shut off and we are awash in the release of tension. The sensation is a chemical rush, an exciting physiological change which our bodies experience as we come down. We associate this feeling with relief, triumph, celebration. We look at our fellow pre-language, proto-humans as we vocalize our gasps of relief—do you feel this too? Did you see the looks on our faces? We just faced danger and we kicked ass! Take that, unexpected shadow on the wall! We are superior!

Is it any wonder that we'd start seeking out this feeling?

It's possible that even to this day, the recognition of safe incongruity flips trace-level switches in us—just a quick on and off—and we've held onto the laugh as a response to the flicker. Of course, the incongruity must be high enough to warrant the response, or be accompanied by emotional enhancers to strengthen the signal. (Obviously, if the event triggers too many inhibitors, the whole deal is off. Inhibitors may threaten the "safety" with which we view incongruity.)

This also fits in with the idea that surprise is a powerful element in comedy—when we are startled we go through the same rapid high-alert/cool-down process. It's not uncommon for people to have scrapes with death and then, finding themselves unharmed, to start laughing. Likewise, it's common for people to be startled during a horror film and then turn to each other and laugh.

Our ability to safely create the rush has evolved with our cognitive development. Now we employ complex linguistic and dramatic structures to create and sustain safe incongruity. Jokes are like puzzles, and the reward for solving them is the present-day recognition of incongruity. We feel a similar celebratory high.

Laughter as behavioral emoticon

But there is an important element here: sharing. If laughter was pre-language, it is reasonable to wonder if we have appropriated the sound of our own laughter and given it a second purpose, that of communication—the recognition of play, a show of appreciation. We take that sound which we all associate with joy and use it to disarm, to put each other at ease. This is the vocal equivalent of wagging our tails. It's the behavioral emoticon: the literal LOL.

How often have we laughed just to be nice? Or primarily because we love the person trying to be funny? Or because we were all having such a gosh darn great time? Yet later, we examine the things we were laughing at and realize they aren't all that funny.

We can visualize the two types of laughter as in (Figure 1.1):

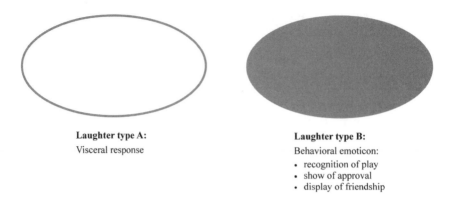

Laughter type A:
Visceral response

Laughter type B:
Behavioral emoticon:
- recognition of play
- show of approval
- display of friendship

In comedy—particularly live comedy—both laughs are important. It is often difficult to distinguish between these two responses, as they've become so entwined. Indeed, as we laugh at the content of a funny joke we may also be laughing to show appreciation of the source (Figure 1.2):

Laughter types A +B

Either laugh-type can dominate the response. I attended a dinner party at which the host told an amusing story. He got a big laugh from his guests. A few weeks later we were talking about comedy theory and I asked him what accounted for the response. He talked about the structure and surprise ending of his story, and he may have been right, but only to a certain extent. The story was amusing, but not hilarious. What else was going on? He was the host of the party, so he held the social power. He told the story well, to guests who'd been drinking. It was late in the evening, he stood in front of the door, and they were holding their coats. I suspect his laugh was more social than visceral, as shown in (Figure 1.3):

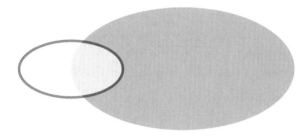

I've also seen this laugh-shape—if I may coin a term—as a response to clever wordplay that does not create any conceptual incongruity. We may also think of this as a head-laugh.

[*Note*: In some theories, wordplay has been characterized as violating the rules of linguistics. This is to prop up the notion that there is a violation making us laugh. However, much wordplay—as we'll see—does not violate rules of linguistics, but works neatly within the rules, in ways that require some cleverness to pull off. The cleverness of the construction elicits appreciation, sometimes expressed as Type B laughter. If the joke manages to also create a concept containing incongruity, Type A will kick in as well.]

We may provoke the inverse of the previous laugh-shape (I think this term is really going to catch on) when we produce high incongruity comedy that is structured more simply—particularly if there is no source physically present. This may be considered more of a gut-laugh, or belly-laugh. (Figure 1.4):

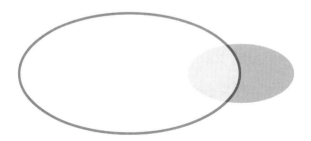

As we'll see in the following chapters, the way in which comedic material is constructed and presented will influence the shape of the laugh.

1.4 EARLY RECEPTION FACTORS

A receiver has enjoyed something amusing and now we want to know which factors were prominent in the shaping of his or her response.

The following chart shows the very beginning of our checklist. The left-hand side documents the nature of the comedic event, while the right-hand side tells us how the receiver responds to each element. The arrows list the variables to be documented.

	ELEMENTS OF COMEDIC EVENT	INFLUENCE ON RECEIVER
RECEIVER PROFILE	baseline reception factors physical state preexisting mood	
ADDITIONAL RECEIVER ROLES		

The receiver profile

Baseline reception factors

People don't come to comedy as blank slates. Each of us has life experiences and preferences that color the way we take in humor. This creates a set of pre-joke reception factors, or baseline reception factors.

If we were going to apply this chart to an actual comedic event, we'd start by putting together a receiver profile. After all, just who is this person? We would want to make a note of basic statistical indicators (gender, age, education level, area of residence, etc.) and psychological indicators (personality surveys, history of comedic preferences. etc).

Physical state

Now we look at the receiver at the time of the event, beginning with physical state. Obviously, if one doesn't feel well, one may not be as ready to laugh as someone who is in good health. Conversely, there are physical conditions, such as overtiredness or drunkenness, that can influence the willingness to take part in comedy.

Pre-existing mood

Likewise, the pre-existing mood of the receiver is worth noting. One may simply not be in the mood to laugh. Conversely, someone in a giddy mood may laugh hysterically at the mildest joke.

Before moving on, I notice that the kid in the back of the room has a question. He wants to know if we should be noting minutiae, like weather or degree of sleepiness.

Good one, kid in the back. After all, a person can be affected by weather, right? Should we take that into account? Or time of day? Can a joke told on Christmas day get a different response than the same joke told on the hottest day of the year? Is Saturday night more fun than Sunday morning? What if the receiver is wearing pajamas as opposed to a tuxedo? What about sea level? Where does it all stop?

Yes, all of these elements may contribute to a receiver's physical state and his or her mood. However, it is not our goal to understand specifically why a person is in a specific state at the time of a joke. That's for the receiver's therapist to work out.

Additional receiver roles

We do not always take in entertainment for the sole purpose of enjoyment. Sometimes we approach it critically. It may be that we have been asked to judge material, or we may be seeking out jokes that are good enough to put on our blog.

Whenever we go into comedy in the role of judge or critic, we are likely to be a little harder on the comedy; we're not only taking it in; we're weighing it against other possible material, we're dissecting it, or we're overly aware of our own reaction. The joke now has a heavier burden—our endorsement will say something about our tastes. Others may judge us by how we judge jokes.

The role of critic also comes with a certain amount of power, and power can corrupt, even when it comes to comedy.

I've seen the role of critic skew the results of sitcom testing. There have been members of test audiences who feel the need to expound about what works and doesn't work, out of an apparent need to feel knowledgeable. They may also feel that they have some control over what gets on the air and what doesn't. Then there are those whose criticism is enhanced by the viewers' desire to "get back" at the medium for the years of garbage they've had to endure on television.

If we were documenting an event in which the receiver approached comedy in a critical role, we would need to determine whether the role had any noticeable effect on his or her attitude toward the comedy.

As with any reception factor, though, the receiver may not be aware that anything affected his or her response. If we were mad comedy scientists, we could also chart the receiver's reactions to similar comedy where he or she has no additional receiver roles and look for differences.

1.5 LEVELS OF SOCIAL INTERACTION

Now that we've learned a little about the receiver, we will dig deeper into the scene of the crime and find out if there were any witnesses. As the great comedy detective Werner Heisenberg noted, the very presence of witnesses changes the nature of the joke's outcome.

To determine the level of social interaction, we simply have to answer two questions:

1   During the event, can the receiver communicate with other receivers?

2   During the event, can the receiver communicate with the source of the comedy?

The combined answers can have a huge impact on the way in which comedy is experienced.

How levels of social interaction can influence the receiver

As discussed earlier in this chapter, laughter can have more than one purpose. Aside from being a simple reaction to how funny we find a joke, laughter may be used to communicate approval to a source or a desire to connect with other receivers. We may also use it to show derision or to identify ourselves as part of a group. We may wish to use the sound as acknowledgment of play, even when we don't find actual humor in the playing. This "Type B laugh" can play a major role in our ultimate response.

Communicating with other receivers

We are in a crowded movie theater, laughing our heads off at a comedy. Interestingly, the same movie is playing in another theater where one person constitutes the audience. Chances are, that person is not laughing as much as we are. He's missing out on a great social interaction. We're enjoying laughter as a way to communicate with other receivers, bonding through shared experience.

The effect can be even more potent when the audience is made up of friends or family. Every joke could tip off a series of inside references that you can share with your group, increasing the response. Likewise, the reaction of a group of students to a joke may be different at the beginning of a term, when they're all strangers, than at the end, when they've had some level of bonding.

On the other hand, communication between receivers can also dampen the experience. Imagine you're at a comedy club with some drunken, overenthusiastic friends. While the experience has been heightened for them, your annoyance may dampen the event for you.

When a comedy club audience is small and spread out around the room, the manager will often encourage everyone to sit close together, front and center. He does this to maximize the communication potential not only with other receivers, but also with the source.

Communicating with the source

Someone has told you a joke, or has performed something funny for your amusement. Now he waits for a response. Your degree of laughter will be interpreted by the source as acceptance or rejection. You are not simply receiving; you are taking part in a social interaction. If you wish him to continue telling jokes—say, it's a dull day at the bank—you may laugh harder at the joke than the joke actually warrants, because you are, in effect, asking the source to continue. A small, dismissive laugh may suffice to shut the guy up without being totally rude.

There is also potential for hurtful communication, such as when the source is unintentionally funny and laughter would result in hurt feelings or anger. (Ever get scolded by someone and all you wanted to do was laugh? The need to suppress laughter may actually enhance the hilarity of the moment.)

Even in text conversations, we may still experience low-level pressure to respond to jokes, whether with the simple LOL, or the effusive ROFLMAO (rolling on the floor laughing my ass off). The source's continued attempts at humor will be influenced by your tapping of the keys.

During a live performance, the audience has the potential to communicate with a source. A great amount of laughter can be created in order to encourage and show appreciation to the performer. Notice how effortlessly a crowd's laughter will slide into applause.

Each audience, in my experience, develops its own group identity. There are even dominant laughers who communicate the tenor of the evening to other receivers. Likewise, I've seen a well-timed groan from a single audience member dampen the beginnings of a big laugh. If an individual is susceptible to the group's mood, he or her may find himself laughing (or not laughing) based on what the mob feels rather than the individual's own tastes.

The four levels of social interaction

We determine the level of social interaction in a comedic event by answering the two questions posed at the beginning of this chapter. Since each question can be answered yes or no, there are four possible combinations, and thus four levels.

In each diagram, the arrow represents the direction of communication:

1   *Single receiver, reactive exchange (single/reactive)*

This would be one person, receiving comedy, whether it's printed, audio, visual, or audio-visual comedy. It could also be live comedy via remote technology (Figure 1.5):

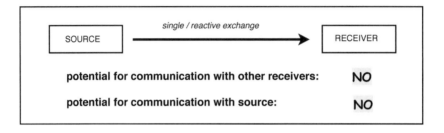

2   *Single receiver, reciprocal exchange (single/reciprocal)*

Somebody tells you a joke or does something funny. You're the only one receiving live comedy, directly from the source. The communication is two-way (Figure 1.6):

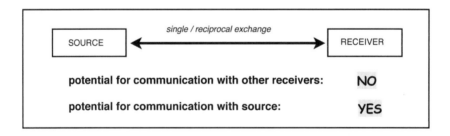

Once we get to multiple receivers, the potential for communication (represented by the arrows) increases significantly.

3   *Multiple receivers, reactive exchange (multiple/reactive)*

This refers to seeing comedy in a crowded movie house. Or two or more people huddled over a book of dirty limericks. Has this happened since 1500? (Figure 1.7):

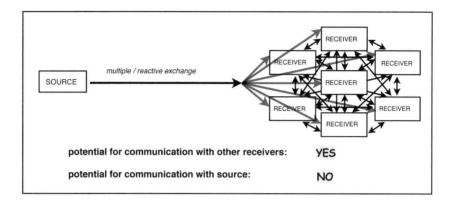

4 *Multiple receivers, reciprocal exchange (multiple/reciprocal)*

This could be a live stage performance. Or a co-worker performing for the office. It's simply in-person comedy done for an audience of more than one (Figure 1.8):

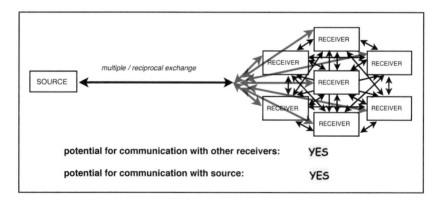

[*Note*: In a reciprocal exchange, the source does not have to address the receiver directly. Characters on stage can make jokes in dialogue with other characters, and the exchange is still reciprocal, in that the receiver can communicate with the source.]

HEY KIDS! TRY THIS AT HOME!

You can experience first hand the effect of social situation on comedy without even leaving the comfort of your living room. It's easy: When you're alone sometime, flip on a TV or computer and watch a sitcom that was filmed in front of a live studio audience. Pick one that you like, something with good characters and great jokes.

Chances are, you won't be laughing as loudly as the studio audience. In fact, they seem to be screaming with laughter at things that only make us smile. Often, people make the assumption that there's a laugh track, but I assure you, most of those laughs are genuine. And they're not wildly out of proportion to the experience the audience is having.

Let's look at the difference. Here's you at home:

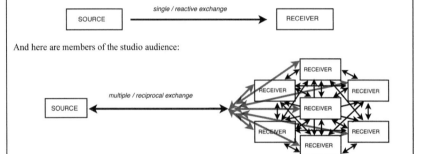

And here are members of the studio audience:

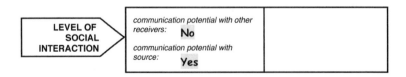

The studio audience has the potential to communicate with other receivers and with the source, while you're all alone with your Jiffy Pop.

Homework for the hardcore comedy detective

In the following examples, five receivers have experienced the same joke, each in very different circumstances. Note the level of social interaction accordingly. The first two are done for you.

1   *Receiver #1* is alone in the car and a friend tells him a joke on his cell phone.

| LEVEL OF SOCIAL INTERACTION | communication potential with other receivers: **No**
 communication potential with source: **Yes** | |

2 *Receiver #2* is in traffic across town and reads the same joke on a bumper sticker.

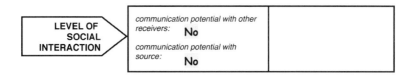

3 *Receiver #3* is with a co-worker. They look out of a seventh-storey window and see a man on the street unwittingly enacting the same joke.

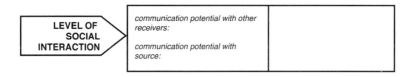

4 *Receiver #4* and 21 other people are conversing in a chatroom and somebody writes the joke in the course of the discussion.

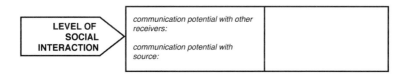

5 *Receiver #5* sees the joke in an Adam Sandler movie at a theater—and Adam Sandler is actually in the audience. (This is a tricky one: answer at the end.)

Answer

Receiver #5: There is communication potential with other receivers and there is communication potential with the source.

2

Elements of communication

2.1 MODES OF COMMUNICATION

Now we start tracking the method in which the joke's information gets into the receiver's head. Below are the basic modes of communication:

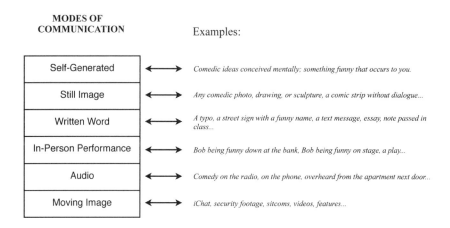

MODES OF COMMUNICATION

Examples:

Self-Generated	*Comedic ideas conceived mentally; something funny that occurs to you.*
Still Image	*Any comedic photo, drawing, or sculpture, a comic strip without dialogue...*
Written Word	*A typo, a street sign with a funny name, a text message, essay, note passed in class...*
In-Person Performance	*Bob being funny down at the bank, Bob being funny on stage, a play...*
Audio	*Comedy on the radio, on the phone, overheard from the apartment next door...*
Moving Image	*iChat, security footage, sitcoms, videos, features...*

For the most part, the examples explain the categories quite nicely. I'll just add a few thoughts.

Self-generated

This refers to the formulation of comedy without outside stimulus. It is not uncommon for a receiver to dream up something funny out of nothing but his own thoughts and mental images.

Still image and written word

The kid in the back, who is forgetting to raise his hand, feels that still image and written word shouldn't be different categories; after all, can't written words be considered as still images?

There is an important difference between the two. The process of reading requires the receiver to decode symbols into words and words into concepts. Understanding a still image doesn't take this kind of deciphering, so the cognitive pressure on the receiver is less.

Of course, these two mediums can work in combination, such as in comic strips. In that case we combine them as written word/still image.

Written words themselves can double as still images for comic effect. By this I mean that they can, by their graphic appearance, induce feelings in a receiver. These feelings can complement or contradict the actual meaning of the words (e.g. a condolence card written in bright, bouncy cartoon letters).

Written words can also appear in video, but unless the words are in motion—and by that I mean dancing around or changing shapes, so that their motion is the joke, rather than their meaning (such as in scrolling)—the mode of communication is the written word, because we are taking in the information through reading.

In-person performance

This could apply to a stand-up comic on stage, just as easily as it could to Grandma telling you a joke over lunch.

The source doesn't have to be intentionally transmitting comedy. He could merely be somebody you spy in a restaurant putting sugar in his coffee one granule at a time. It may be a toddler reacting to something, or a bird flying repeatedly into a window.

The requirement for this category is that the source be in the same physical space with the receiver; there is no technology-based transmission of image or sound.

Moving image and audio

"Moving image" will be taken to mean both silent video footage and sound-augmented video.

Other tactile input

Technically, we can take in comedy through other senses. I know many people to whom the odor of any bodily function is a joke all by itself. We can also taste or touch things we aren't expecting and laugh at the incongruity between expectation and result, or laugh at the implications of the taste or feeling. If Grandma bakes a sugary treat and one bite tells you she used salt instead of sugar, you may laugh at her mistake. Which is rude, considering all she's done for you.

Combination modes

I mentioned that a comic strip may be a combination of still image and written word. This is a combination mode.

There is another way in which we may wish to note more than one mode of communication. Say you're watching a Three Stooges short and you see a sign on the door of a law firm that reads "Dewey, Cheatham, and Howe." The short is in moving image, while the joke is in written word. Likewise, when a comedian like Demetri Martin does stand-up that includes drawings and pictures, we're watching a live performance (or moving image if you're watching it on TV) and a joke that may be still image. Technically, the joke would probably be a combination mode, set up by dialogue in the live performance, and paid off by the graphic.

How mode of communication can influence the receiver

Put simply, there are people who prefer to watch the film *Gone with the Wind* than to slog through the book of the same name. Others love the intricate details in a book that can't be captured on film. Likewise, a receiver may rather see a live performance than watch a video. These preferences, of course, can contribute to the receiver's openness to receiving comedy.

Let's say you love old radio shows on CD—I love Jack Benny, for instance—and someone hands you a CD of Fred Allen, another radio comedian from that era. Your positive experience with audio comedy may increase your level of reception to Mr. Allen.

There are various reasons why a receiver prefers any one mode of communication for entertainment delivery. Here are a few:

- *Time and commitment*: Going back to *Gone with the Wind*, it takes a lot less time to watch the film than it would take to read the entire book. Over the last few generations, receivers seem to prefer getting the gist of the entertainment quickly and moving on to the next idea.

- *Level of decoding*: This is the amount of work it takes for the receiver to translate the incoming information into conceptual ideas. For example, reading the written word requires that the receiver translate squiggles into words. The words themselves are codes for concepts. This takes a higher level of decoding than, say, hearing a joke on the phone, which requires only the translation of sounds into ideas. Still easier is watching a video of Chaplin's character eating a shoe in *The Gold Rush*. In this case we're taking in virtually uncoded information.

Decoding is also determined by whether the comedic idea is shown or told. Audio of a man saying "the dog barked" requires different decoding than audio of a dog barking.

- *Level of sensory reconstruction*: Once we decode the information, we mentally supply what is lacking from the mode of communication. If we read a description of a dog barking, we mentally conjure the sound as well as the visual image. We create surroundings for the dog, time of day, the angle at which we mentally see the animal, etc.

  If we listen to the old Jack Benny program on audio, we supply our own visual universe. And again, we may have to create some of the aural universe, depending on whether concepts are performed vs. described.

  In a play or film, we create the world outside the boundaries of the stage or frame, we fill in the gaps between time dissolves, and, importantly, we eliminate ourselves from the universe; we are there and not there.

Homework for the hardcore comedy detective

In these following examples, five receivers have experienced the same joke in different circumstances. Fill in the provided sections of the chart. The first two are filled in for you.

1 *Receiver #1* hears the joke on a radio commercial as he carpools to work.

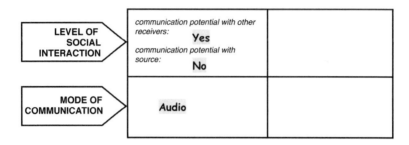

2 *Receiver #2* sees the joke in an animated movie, watched alone on an iPod.

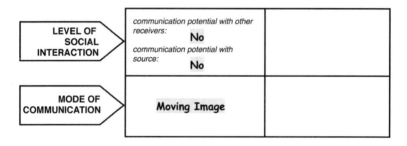

3 *Receiver #3* reads the joke from a Tom Stoppard play in the library.

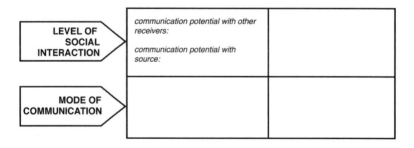

4   *Receiver #4* sees the joke in a Tom Stoppard play in a crowded theater.

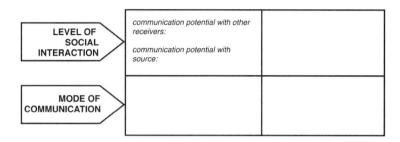

5   *Receiver #5* sees the same joke in a Beetle Bailey comic strip that he
    reads to his kids.

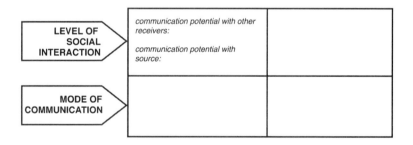

2.2 DEVICE AND SPECIFIC DEVICE

What is a device?

A device is the physical means through which we access comedic information.
It stores and/or plays the information for the receiver.

If you read a funny essay, your mode of communication is the written
word. You may read it in a book, or on a laptop. These are devices. You can

also read it on a T-shirt or a billboard, or on a cereal box or in a very large fortune cookie. All are devices.

Television is a device used for the delivery of moving images. So is a movie theater, an iPhone, or anything that can deliver video to the eyes of the receiver.

It would be virtually impossible to list all the devices for every mode of communication—by the time I'd finish, ten new ones would be on the market—but here are a few examples:

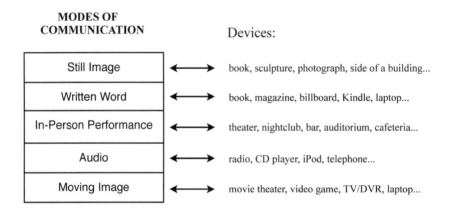

Devices and multiple modes of communication

Obviously, some devices can access more than one mode of communication. The iPhone, for example, can bring you comedy in every mode except that of in-person performance.

Sometimes two devices need to work in tandem to deliver communication, for example, a CD and a laptop.

What is a specific device?

We know you listened to audio comedy on a radio. But which radio? Your new car stereo? An old crystal radio set from the basement? It may be a Zenith Royal 200, or, even more specifically, Dad's old radio from the junk drawer.

The possible relationship between receiver and specific device may actually affect the comedic experience.

How devices can influence the receiver

Preference for devices

Reading a book is a tactile experience; one may enjoy the feel of an old book, the privacy and silence of reading, the smell of the pages. One may enjoy the glossy pages of a magazine less. The same material presented in email may not be as pleasurable. In each case, the receiver takes in written words, but he or she may have a preference for the device in which they are presented.

My daughter prefers to watch TV shows from her laptop as opposed to a TV. Same information, different device. It may be about the convenience, or it's simply a habit she got into at college. Regardless, she now has a preference.

Feelings about specific devices

Imagine this scenario. One day, you're rummaging through a drawer and find an old transistor radio that reminds you of your dad. Now you switch on the transistor radio and listen to some AM morning deejays yukking it up. Putting aside the curious fact that the batteries still work, you may have added another level of enjoyment to this experience. Your delight at finding this radio may increase your level of reception to comedy.

A specific device may also bring negative feelings: a book might be moldy, a laptop might not give you the volume you want, etc.

In another example, a receiver sees a comedy film at a movie theater. The mode of communication is moving image. The device is a movie theater. The specific device is the Arclight Movie Theater in Sherman Oaks, California.

In this situation, the receiver may have a preference for seeing films in movie theaters. He or she may also have feelings associated with this particular theater.

Remember the first time you saw something on a flat-screen TV or on an iPhone? The novelty of this specific device may have increased your openness to being entertained.

I see that the kid in the back has a question. He wants to know if all these reception factors carry the same weight—does a receiver's preference for TV over a laptop matter as much as, say, the level of communication in the comedic event?

Good question. (Why can't more of you be like the kid in the back?) There will be some factors that definitely outweigh others in importance. In the grand scheme of things, I can't imagine that the specific device will very often be the primary factor behind a laugh. But it's not unheard of.

Homework for the hardcore comedy detective

Once again, five receivers experience the same joke, with different elements of context and transmission:

1   *Receiver #1*, alone, sees the joke acted out in the feature "Spy vs. Spy" in a *Mad Magazine* from his attic.

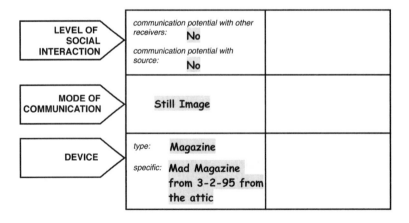

2   *Receiver #2* witnesses the same joke happening to someone in a YouTube video. He watches it with his friends on his iPhone.

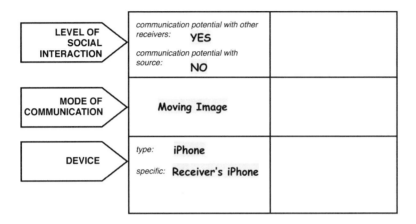

LEVEL OF SOCIAL INTERACTION	communication potential with other receivers: **YES** communication potential with source: **NO**	
MODE OF COMMUNICATION	**Moving Image**	
DEVICE	type: **iPhone** specific: **Receiver's iPhone**	

3   *Receiver #3* sees it in a Harold Lloyd film with a large crowd at the Cinema 20 Theater.

LEVEL OF SOCIAL INTERACTION	communication potential with other receivers: communication potential with source:	
MODE OF COMMUNICATION		
DEVICE	type: specific:	

4   *Receiver #4* hears the joke described on an old Smothers Brothers album from Grandpa's collection, played on his favorite record player at his wake.

LEVEL OF SOCIAL INTERACTION	*communication potential with other receivers:* *communication potential with source:*	
MODE OF COMMUNICATION		
DEVICE	*type:* *specific:*	

5   *Receiver #5* is sitting on a bus, and sees the joke on a billboard on the side of the old Cleveland Trust Building.

LEVEL OF SOCIAL INTERACTION	*communication potential with other receivers:* *communication potential with source:*	
MODE OF COMMUNICATION		
DEVICE	*type:* *specific:*	

3

Vehicles

3.1 VEHICLES

A vehicle is a man-made creative construct in which a joke may appear.

There are many types of vehicles. Some, like plays, films, novels, sitcoms, and sketches, create a narrative context for the joke. Others are non-narrative, being merely collections of jokes that have been packaged and presented to the masses. The presented collection is the vehicle.

[*Note*: The device is the physical container for the comedy. The vehicle is the creative container. In the written word, a book would be a device (physical container) and a novel would be a vehicle (creative container).]

In short, a vehicle:

1 Is a man-made, prepared creative construct.

2 May provide a larger creative context for the joke.

3 Is presented to the masses.

4 Has known rules of presentational structure (the vehicle's language).

Obviously, this is a broad enough set of qualities to cover everything from a historical novel to a greeting card. As we'll see, however, the existence and nature of a vehicle profoundly affects the mindset with which we encounter the jokes within.

Overview: Vehicular and non-vehicular comedy

Here is an example of the non-vehicular joke (Figure 3.1):

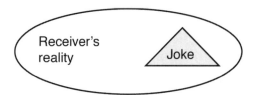

This joke can spring from the immediate reality of the receiver, such as a snarky comment overheard in a restaurant or something funny said during a phone conversation, or witnessed on the street. It can also appear in the form of a stand-alone joke. This is any joke that does not come in a larger creative or presentational package. When your friend Bob says, "So a guy walks into a bar ..." he is delivering a joke that is unattached to a vehicle.

Compare this with a joke that appears in the middle of an episode of *I Love Lucy*. The joke here has no relation to the immediate reality of the receiver. It springs instead from the world of its immediate vehicle, in this case a sitcom. The receiver's feelings about sitcoms in general (and this episode specifically) will influence his or her esponse to the joke (Figure 3.2):

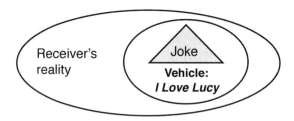

We also find vehicles-within-vehicles. A receiver may have feelings about the outer vehicle, in this case *Saturday Night Live*, but then have very different feelings about the immediate vehicle, any sketch within. Feelings for each vehicle may affect the receiver's openness to comedy. And how's this for a vehicle within a vehicle? Stephen King used to publish short stories in men's magazines like *Cavalier* and *Gent*. I've got to wonder how feelings for those content providers influenced the readers' perceptions of his stories (Figure 3.3):

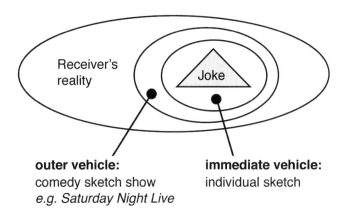

outer vehicle:
comedy sketch show
e.g. Saturday Night Live

immediate vehicle:
individual sketch

Vehicular intent, non-vehicular response: the blooper and ironic comedy

Imagine you're going to see a high school production of *Grease* with your 10-year-old child. The production is shoddy but your kid is really into it. He is laughing at vehicular comedy. On the other hand, you may be laughing for entirely different reasons; the acting is bad, the songs are off-key, etc. You may be laughing where you're supposed to laugh, but your pleasure is rooted in your own reality as opposed to the reality of the vehicle. Your response is non-vehicular.

The same thing happens when we laugh at bad low-budget films or laugh because actors in old movies are smoking so much. Our response is rooted in our reality rather than the vehicle's. The comedy is unintentional.

Unintentional comedy can occur in the form of a mistake on the stage or a typo on the page. Each one of these situations, in effect, yanks us back into our own reality. We don't find a typo in a book and assume Tom Sawyer numbered the pages wrong. We know the culprit was someone in our world.

Then we have bloopers on TV. If a studio audience witnesses actors making mistakes during a performance the comedy is non-vehicular. When these mistakes are packaged and presented on TV as mass entertainment they have been rendered vehicular. The packaging creates the vehicular framework for the bloopers.

ANECDOTE ALERT

In an episode of *The Mary Tyler Moore Show* called "Lou Dates Mary," Mary and her boss decide to go on a date. Things are awkward, and at the climax they lean in for a kiss—and then both start laughing at the ridiculousness of trying to move the friendship onto anything more than it was.

When Lou and Mary start laughing at the crucial moment it's funny, and the studio audience laughs. But the laugh is odd. It starts out as a shriek and then tapers quickly. When I first saw it on TV many years ago, there was something about the laugh that felt kind of off, kind of unsatisfying.

Years later I put a joke in a joke in an episode of *Cheers* where Norm starts talking about turning his life around and getting a real job—but he's only joking and can't finish the line without laughing. On the night of the filming, the studio audience watched Norm crack himself up and they laughed—the same laugh I'd heard years earlier on *Mary Tyler Moore*: a shriek and then a rapid decline.

In that moment I figured it out. In both cases the actors laughed mid-line or in mid-scene, and the studio audience thought they were witnessing a blooper. They thought the actors had forgotten their lines. So the audience has a loud laugh, but as the scene continues they realize their mistake and have to be quiet so as to jump back into the show's reality.

The audience at home could never make that mistake. Bloopers are not shown in the course of sitcoms. They are shown outside the world of the sitcom, on blooper compilations or as separate clips.

Vehicles and in-person performance

Obviously, sketches and plays are vehicles. But what about monologues? Is there a difference between a comedian telling jokes on stage and your co-worker cracking jokes on your coffee break?

Absolutely. Below is the difference in diagram form. First, our friend Bob gets on a roll at work or at a party (Figure 3.4):

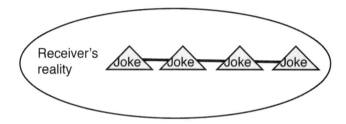

Now let's see Bob's act as a formally presented vehicle (Figure 3.5):

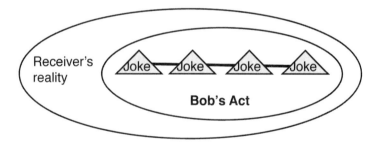

The difference is more than an extra circle drawn around some triangles. Turning these jokes into an act changes the way you take them in. It also changes the nature of your relationship to Bob.

The wall between receiver and vehicle

A vehicle creates an invisible wall between the source and the receiver. This wall, in effect, transforms the receiver from an individual to part of an audience. The wall is created and reinforced in a number of ways.

- *Announcement*: The simplest way to inform the receiver that a vehicle is coming is to announce it. The announcement can be as simple as a title. If you read something funny that was part of an email to you, the joke is non-vehicular. Email between you and a friend keeps you on an equal footing; the interchange is based in your reality. Often, however, your friend will forward you some kind of titled mass email, like "You Know You're Over The Hill When …." The title alerts us that we may be heading for a vehicle; material created for consumption by the masses.

  The announcement can also be a literal announcement. If you're at a kid's birthday party and the host announces that Bingo the Clown is going to do his act, the partygoers will arrange themselves into an audience. At early ages, we are taught our social role as the recipients of live entertainment.

- *Inequality between receivers and source: an individual becomes audience*: When a comedian is on stage, look at the physical arrangement we all assume. He stands in front of everyone, in a space reserved for his performance. Everyone else is gathered and seated, facing this one person. This is not the normal way in which people interact. It is a specific social construction, built for the reception of information.

  The audience is aware of their role. They are not on equal footing with the performer. It is ingrained in us to know that the person in front is spreading information among the multitude, and therefore has social control. This is also true of the classroom—a lecture may be said to be a vehicle.

What does it mean to change into an audience? In live comedy, when a receiver becomes an audience, that receiver sacrifices his or her identity. It is understood that the individual is now a generic part of a larger entity, an entity that can exist without any one person.

Even a single person watching television or reading a novel is an audience. He or she knows that the program is not communicating with him or her, but to a larger entity of which the receiver is part.

- *Mass-directed content*: As receivers, we recognize that vehicular comedy is designed or presented for the masses.

Imagine that your friend emails you an amusing video clip of himself eating ravioli until he throws up. This is non-vehicular comedy. Even if he titles it. It is simply the video equivalent of someone telling you a funny story about himself.

Now imagine he sends the same clip in a mass email to a group consisting of family and friends. This is still non-vehicular comedy. It is understood that each recipient has a relationship with the source and is on equal footing with the source.

Now the guy posts the video on YouTube. It is available for the masses—the generic audience with whom he has no relationship. They are simply looking for entertainment, and for whatever reason they may click on Matt's Ravioli Binge. They may find it amusing (turning it into a viral success story), or not. These people are the masses; the comedy has become vehicular.

[*Note*: Comedy can be made vehicular by someone other than the source of comedy. Any receiver can find an old video and turn it into a comedic vehicle for mass consumption.]

Interactivity: blurring the line between receiver and source

Long before the Internet, there were vehicles that were built for interactivity. Mad Libs is an example, as is improv-based stage comedy. On TV and radio, there have been call-in shows since the dawn of time. And now we have the Internet, on which anyone can create material or reshape the material of others.

How does all this affect the wall between source and audience?

It's still there. Many websites are designed to be added to by individual receivers. Does this mean the content is co-created by the audience? On the contrary: a receiver separates him- or herself from the audience in order to take on the role of co-source. This is the equivalent of an audience member running up onto the stage to tell a joke for the masses.

How many individuals does it take to constitute "the masses"?

Changing things further, we have applications like Facebook and Twitter allowing us to turn strangers into "friends." When you put up posts for your 900 friends, are you performing for the masses? At what number does this occur?

Here we run into the age-old question of how many grains of sand before we have a beach. If we try dealing in numbers we'll get tangled up. Also, let's be clear: Facebook does not really turn strangers into friends as much as it turns friends (and strangers) into an audience. When we post a joke we are doing so for an audience. When people comment they become sources as well, since their comments are public.

If Facebook posts and tweets are vehicles, they are certainly vehicles of the lowest possible wattage. The only formal announcement may be the banner of "Facebook" or "Twitter" itself. Posts require only the most basic rules of structure or content. We know how easy it is for the source to throw random thoughts out there, and for receivers it takes little effort to read what they say.

So what is the comedy detective to do? For now, Facebook posts and tweets and website comments and the like can all be noted as vehicles, with the understanding that we are dancing on the line between vehicular and non-vehicular comedy.

Content providers

As we've seen, vehicles can exist within vehicles. A sketch on *Saturday Night Live*, for example. And in Cleveland, *Saturday Night Live* is broadcast on WKYC TV, which is an affiliate of NBC.

WKYC and NBC themselves are forms of vehicles. They are content providers.

They are vehicles because they have a public identity; a creative public interface that is maintained through written copy, unifying visuals, promos, on-air staff, and executive decision making. These vehicles are like ringmasters at a never-ending circus, bringing us a parade of smaller, self-contained vehicles, one after another.

One aspect of content providers is that they are only destinations for receivers because of the vehicles within. No one watches NBC to watch the NBC public interface. Likewise, no one goes to YouTube (another content provider) to watch YouTube. They go to watch videos. Yet YouTube has its own public interface; it communicates to its users, selects videos to spotlight, and uses a basic amount of gatekeeping.

Different content providers have different levels of gatekeeping. YouTube displays such a wide range of content that there is no unifying creative vision from one video to the next. They pretty much keep their hands off the videos, barring only those which are illegal to show.

Other content providers, like NBC, are more hands-on with their gatekeeping, being sure to choose vehicles that help define the creative vision of the network overall.

Even more hands-on are magazines. They not only publish regular features that reflect and reinforce a specific style, tone, and point of view, they also include their own self-generated vehicles. The magazine "speaks" to us directly through editorial pieces and the like. We get to know the staff of Esquire or that usual gang of idiots at *Mad*.

How vehicles can influence the receiver

Let's go back to Bob down at the bank. He makes the day go faster by telling jokes. Inevitably, someone says, "Hey, Bob, you've got to do this professionally!" Sure enough, at the next amateur night, Bob goes on stage and does his act exactly as he does down at the vault. And he bombs. Assuming he didn't just get a bad audience, why might this be the case?

Bob tried to transfer comedy that succeeded at one level (non-vehicular) to another (vehicular) without appreciating the primary difference:

Expectations are higher for vehicular comedy.

Comedy that is non-vehicular is like a gift. We encounter it casually, and we're happy to get it. But what happens when you bring those same jokes to a comedy club where people gave up their free time to drive there, paid a cover charge, and had to applaud when you were introduced?

Bob's jokes went from a no-pressure context to a high-pressure context.

I see this all the time. People will see a joke on a sitcom and roll their eyes, while the same joke told by a relative at dinner will have them clutching their sides.

The other thing I hear constantly is this one: "Hey, you want an idea for a show? Just spend a day at the office with me. Those guys are funnier than any sitcom. I mean, they're all hysterical. You have no idea!"

Yes I do. And your office is not a good sitcom. No offense—I'm sure life there is hysterical in non-vehicular form. But adapting it to a vehicle is an enormous challenge.

Earlier, I mentioned the vehicle's language. Some of these languages are so familiar to us that when we experience a vehicle like a sitcom or a novel we are unaware of how stylized it is, how different it is from language we use in our lives. If an actual half-hour of TV were to show people as they really speak, with all the "um's" and the dramatically pointless cycles of repeat phrases and meandering topics, we would find it almost unbearable to watch. Have you ever noticed that no one on a scripted program ever gets to sneeze unless it's a part of the plot?

The language of a vehicle is not limited to the verbal. In film, we understand what it means to cut to different angles, or dissolve to later times. In a one-panel cartoon we know where the caption goes, what word and thought balloons mean, as well as other conventions that might come into play.

As a postscript to the plight of poor Bob, I've seen people make the exact opposite mistake. A comedian friend of mine occasionally tries to shoehorn material into his conversations, hijacking the exchange and trying to turn innocent receivers into audience members. His friends/audience will laugh politely, but they feel that wall being put up and it sometimes makes them uncomfortable; their equal footing has been taken away.

ANECDOTE ALERT

Here is a miscalculation by a writer who worked on the show *Cheers*. This series takes place in a bar, and the writer went out to a real bar one night hoping to get ideas for the show. There he saw one guy challenge another to remember all the words to the song "Hot Rod Lincoln." The challenged barfly started reciting the lyrics, and the challenger joined in. Soon there were a bunch of guys rattling off the words to this song while people kept the beat by pounding tables and the bar. Faster and faster, louder and louder this thing went, the tension building as no one left out a syllable. The whole bar was absorbed in this now speeding train. When the song came to its conclusion, the whole place went nuts. Whooping, clapping, laughing.

▶

The next day this writer came in, all a-buzz. He had to get this into a *Cheers* episode.

When the script containing this real-life incident made it to the table and the actors read it aloud for the first time, the bit died. It not only died, but it died for three excruciating pages—an eternity for the writer.

The writer made the same mistake as Bob down at the bank.

An event like the "Hot Rod Lincoln" challenge can be a highlight of comedy among people who are slightly drunk, slightly bored, and know each other pretty well. Their laughter was specific and appropriate to the reality in which it was generated. The same incident won't be a comedy highlight in a sitcom populated by witty characters whose every word comes from the pens of Emmy-winning writers.

Expectations are raised in relation to the nature of the vehicle

The standards to which we hold vehicular comedy vary from vehicle to vehicle. Among the contributing factors for this are:

- *Awareness of presentational effort*: We are always somewhat aware of the amount of effort it took to put a vehicle in front of us. We may hold a polished sitcom to a higher standard than we would a clip of someone's home movies that were slapped up on YouTube with minimal time and effort.

  Even so, we have (at least incrementally) higher standards for a YouTube video than for non-vehicular comedy. A YouTube video has to have been selected and uploaded. Clearly the uploader believes his or her material is at least good enough to warrant the time and energy it takes to put it out there.

- *Expectation of gatekeeping*: Gatekeeping refers to the selection of material presented for public consumption. We assume that every vehicle has gone through some sort of selection process. We expect more stringent levels of gatekeeping from Hollywood than we do from some high school student posting homemade cartoons on the Internet. And even with the teenage cartoonist, we might hope for some small amount of discretion in what he or she chooses to exhibit.

- *Requirements on the part of the receiver*: A vehicle like a comic strip can be enjoyed at a glance within ten seconds. A YouTube video takes a click and a few minutes. A play demands that we get dressed and go out for the evening. As requirements for the receiver increase, we may hold the comedy to higher standards—we are being told that the material is worthy of our time and effort.

When the presence of a vehicle raises expectations, receivers can be affected in a couple of ways. Sometimes it triggers a challenge: "Okay, I'm going to spend time here: make me laugh." Increased production value can have the same effect: "You're working pretty hard here, this had better be hilarious."

Conversely, receivers may be fooled into thinking that mediocre material is funnier because it appears in a polished product. Plays, for example, are often regarded with more respect than sitcoms. Perhaps it's because sitcoms are free and disposable, whereas with a play the receiver has to make a reservation, plop down money, and leave his home. Something about being required to do all this increases the amount of respect the receiver has for the form. I've seen jokes that would have gotten groans from a sitcom audience get huge laughs on a theater stage.

Expectation and hype

Hype is a double-edged sword. On the one hand, it can actually fool people into believing a vehicle is better than it is. On the other, it can lead to disappointment.

We've all been through this one. Our friends tell us we have to go see some movie or read some book because it's the funniest thing ever, and they guarantee (guarantee!) we'll love it. And we go, and it's nowhere near as good as the hype, so we're disappointed. Conversely, we may avoid a film because everyone hates it. Then, one afternoon, we catch it on TV and it's not bad at all.

Then there's my friend the contrarian. If something is popular with the public, then he believes it cannot be any good. And so he encounters the vehicle with a predisposition for not liking it.

I attended college at a time when everyone walked around doing lines from *Monty Python's Flying Circus* in bad English accents. All the time. And they thought they were being hilarious. Have I impressed upon you that this happened all the time? I grew to hate many of these people. So, of course, when I started watching the program, I had to overcome my feelings about these people before I could appreciate how absolutely brilliant the show was.

TANGENT ALERT 1: THE DUAL NATURE OF THE SITCOM

I'm not going to be too strict about this, but it's good to know: there are two kinds of sitcoms and they could technically be considered separate vehicles.

The shot-in-front-of-a-studio-audience-on-a-stage kind (the multi-camera sitcom) is descended from the stage. In fact, it looks like a filmed play (*Two and a Half Men, Everybody Loves Raymond, Cheers, The Mary Tyler Moore Show, Dick Van Dyke, I Love Lucy*, etc.).

The single-camera sitcom is descended from film. The scenes are shot out of sequence, and with no audience present (*Modern Family, The Office, Malcom in the Middle, The Wonder Years, M*A*S*H*, Gilligan's Island*, etc.).

The difference may seem small, but the effect on our viewing is huge.

Single-camera shows can employ every level of comedy, whether it's meant to elicit a smile or a chuckle or a hearty bellow. The audience can have all those reactions and the comedy is successful. You could watch an episode of *The Office* and appreciate many comedy levels and not even laugh out loud.

In a sitcom with a studio audience, things get stickier. The audience at home is keenly aware of the presence of the studio audience on the soundtrack. So let's say the writers throw in a joke that's meant to elicit a smile. In *The Office*, this joke may elicit a smile from people watching at home. In our studio audience show, however, the same mild joke bombs, and it bombs big time. Why? The viewers at home hear something that sounds like a joke, and then they hear the deafening silence of an audience not laughing. They got no confirmation from the studio audience that this material was funny. And so it looks like a joke that tried and failed. And so nobody smiles, least of all the network executives.

On a studio audience show, the writers can only aim for the types of dialogue and situations that will elicit a big response from the studio audience. Any mid-level joke will only get a mid-level response from the studio audience, and, again, it'll look like a joke that tried and failed.

TANGENT ALERT 2: VIOLATING THE LANGUAGE OF THE VEHICLE

Let's look at Bonnie Hunt, who, as of this writing, has had three studio audience sitcoms on air. In my opinion she made the same mistake every time: she put on shows that were largely improvised. While some critics were charmed by her daring, the results were ultimately unsatisfying.

An improv show is a vehicle with very different rules than a sitcom. An improv audience will sit through long stretches of tedium and bad scene structure just to enjoy those flashes of brilliance that come from the players.

But the television audience expected a sitcom. These viewers were not ready for long stretches of an audience not laughing. In a theater, her show might get a standing ovation every night and be heralded as fantastic improvisational humor, but her show was packaged as a sitcom, and the sound of a studio audience quietly appreciating was still the sound of an audience not laughing. In short, she violated the language of the sitcom.

This would close the book on the matter, but for a successful sitcom called *Curb Your Enthusiasm*. Each episode is mapped out in detail, but

▶

then the scenes are improvised. Does this mean that Larry David and his cast are better at improvising than Bonnie Hunt and her cast? Not necessarily. *Curb Your Enthusiasm* is a single-camera show. Every level of comedy is possible (see Tangent alert 1). Bonnie Hunt lived and died by audience laughter.

Specific vehicles

While a vehicle is a type of mass entertainment, a specific vehicle is the individually identified entertainment which falls within that type. For example, a sitcom is a type of vehicle, while an episode of *I Love Lucy* called "Lucy Thinks Ricky is Trying to Murder Her" (wonder what that one's about) is a specific vehicle.

A novel is a vehicle, while *The Great Gatsby* is a specific vehicle.

This chart offers a way of looking at a specific vehicle:

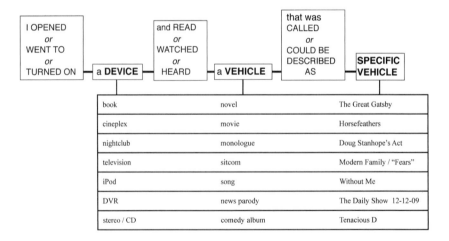

I OPENED *or* WENT TO *or* TURNED ON — a **DEVICE**	and READ *or* WATCHED *or* HEARD — a **VEHICLE**	that was CALLED *or* COULD BE DESCRIBED AS — **SPECIFIC VEHICLE**
book	novel	The Great Gatsby
cineplex	movie	Horsefeathers
nightclub	monologue	Doug Stanhope's Act
television	sitcom	Modern Family / "Fears"
iPod	song	Without Me
DVR	news parody	The Daily Show 12-12-09
stereo / CD	comedy album	Tenacious D

Another way to look at vehicles is shown in Figure 3.6:

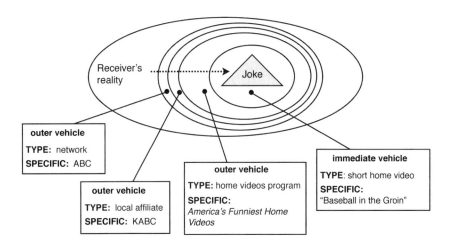

In this example, a receiver is responding to a joke from a video on *America's Funniest Home Videos.* The video is the joke's immediate vehicle. If the receiver were responding to a joke made by the host of the show, then *America's Funniest Home Videos* would be the immediate vehicle.

If the video were seen on YouTube, it would resemble Figure 3.7:

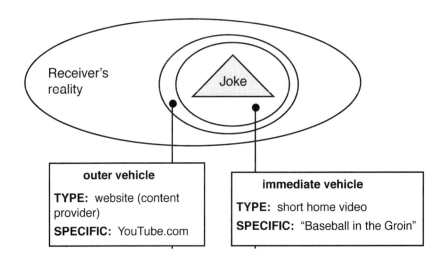

How specific vehicles can influence the receiver

A receiver's preference for a specific vehicle can color the way he or she reacts to the humor within.

This is something I saw all the time while I wrote for *Frasier*. We weren't above doing some pretty silly jokes now and again, but the show had such a stellar reputation that viewers who usually sniffed at the same jokes on *Three's Company* would go around quoting us the next day.

Homework for the hardcore comedy detective

Note: *Don't drive yourself crazy*: Many vehicles have well-known classifications, such as "essay" or "sitcom." There are dozens of recognizable man-made creative constructs, however, that do not have formal names. Any handy generic description will do. The regular feature "Humor In Uniform" in *Readers Digest* could simply be a "recurring humorous feature." On the Internet, we may find a "humor-based website" or "interactive site" or "website of user-supplied content." What's important is whether or not the receiver recognizes the vehicle type and has any feelings or preferences one way or another about it.

Here is an example of a vehicle within a vehicle:

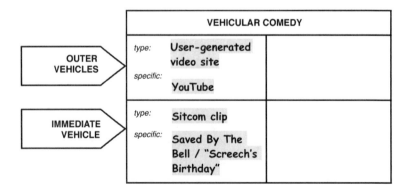

Five receivers have encountered the same basic joke in five different sets of circumstances.

1   *Receiver #1* finds the joke in the library's copy of *Tom Sawyer*.

	ELEMENTS OF COMEDIC EVENT	INFLUENCE ON RECEIVER
RECEIVER PROFILE	*baseline reception factors* *physical state* *preexisting mood*	
ADDITIONAL RECEIVER ROLES	None	
LEVEL OF SOCIAL INTERACTION	*communication potential with other receivers:* No *communication potential with source:* No	
MODE OF COMMUNICATION	Written Word	
DEVICE	*type:* Book *specific:* Library Book	

	VEHICULAR COMEDY	
OUTER VEHICLES	*type:* None *specific:*	
IMMEDIATE VEHICLE	*type:* Novel *specific:* Tom Sawyer	

2 *Receiver #2* sees it in a Brewster Rockit comic strip, read from the receiver's *LA Times* on a bus.

	ELEMENTS OF COMEDIC EVENT	INFLUENCE ON RECEIVER
RECEIVER PROFILE	*baseline reception factors* *physical state* *preexisting mood*	
ADDITIONAL RECEIVER ROLES	None	
LEVEL OF SOCIAL INTERACTION	*communication potential with other receivers:* No *communication potential with source:* No	
MODE OF COMMUNICATION	Still Image / Written Word	
DEVICE	*type:* Newspaper *specific:* Receiver's paper	

	VEHICULAR COMEDY	
OUTER VEHICLES	*type:* Newspaper *specific:* LA Times	
IMMEDIATE VEHICLE	*type:* Comic strip *specific:* Brewtser Rockit	

3 *Receiver #3* hears it on Comedy Central's *The Daily Show*, watched on the living-room TV with the family.

	ELEMENTS OF COMEDIC EVENT	INFLUENCE ON RECEIVER
RECEIVER PROFILE	baseline reception factors physical state preexisting mood	
ADDITIONAL RECEIVER ROLES		
LEVEL OF SOCIAL INTERACTION	communication potential with other receivers: communication potential with source:	
MODE OF COMMUNICATION		
DEVICE	type: specific:	

	VEHICULAR COMEDY	
OUTER VEHICLES	type: specific:	
IMMEDIATE VEHICLE	type: specific:	

4 *Receiver #4* catches it in a stage production of *Tom Sawyer* from the fourth row at the Plymouth Theater on Broadway.

	ELEMENTS OF COMEDIC EVENT	INFLUENCE ON RECEIVER
RECEIVER PROFILE	baseline reception factors physical state preexisting mood	
ADDITIONAL RECEIVER ROLES		
LEVEL OF SOCIAL INTERACTION	communication potential with other receivers: communication potential with source:	
MODE OF COMMUNICATION		
DEVICE	type: specific:	

	VEHICULAR COMEDY	
OUTER VEHICLES	type: specific:	
IMMEDIATE VEHICLE	type: specific:	

5 *Receiver #5* finds it in a cartoon on *Saturday Night Live*, watched alone on his bedroom TV, broadcast on your local NBC affiliate.

	ELEMENTS OF COMEDIC EVENT	INFLUENCE ON RECEIVER
RECEIVER PROFILE	*baseline reception factors* *physical state* *preexisting mood*	
ADDITIONAL RECEIVER ROLES		
LEVEL OF SOCIAL INTERACTION	*communication potential with other receivers:* *communication potential with source:*	
MODE OF COMMUNICATION		
DEVICE	*type:* *specific:*	

	VEHICULAR COMEDY	
OUTER VEHICLES	*type:* *specific:*	
IMMEDIATE VEHICLE	*type:* *specific:*	

3.2 VEHICLE-BASED RECEPTION FACTORS

In this section we look at two properties of the joke's immediate vehicle and discuss how they can color our reception of the jokes within.

1 Direction of communication

Some vehicles—monologues, for example—are built for the performer to communicate directly to the audience. The performer is aware of the audience's presence and addresses them. Other vehicles, like plays, can be indirect—interaction is observed between characters who do not acknowledge the existence of the audience. This is a kind of fake voyeurism, in which the audience becomes the unseen observer. Then there are dual-exchange vehicles; those plays, films, and TV shows that allow for a narrator or character to address the audience while other characters interact with each other, oblivious to our presence.

How direction of communication can influence the receiver

When someone speaks to us directly, we assume an active role in the communication. When we observe comedy from the interaction of characters who do not acknowledge our presence, we take on a more passive role. In a hybrid vehicle, of course, we take on whatever role is required at any given moment. This is a dual role.

A joke may get some of its humor from breaking the pattern of communication set up by the vehicle. Groucho's breaking of the fourth wall forces us to jump from a passive to an active role. This occurs in a lot of films, of course. Oliver Hardy made it a trademark. Eddie Murphy does one look to the camera—a reaction shot—during *Trading Places* and the moment is unexpected and hilarious. Then there's Ferris Bueller, who talks to us throughout *Ferris Bueller's Day Off*.

I see a familiar hand—it's the kid in the back with another question (does anyone else even pay attention?). He wants to know: How can we have an active role in the comedy if we're watching it on film? Because we're simple creatures, that's why. We merely have to be acknowledged by the performer in order to automatically perk up and listen. Increasing our level of attention when we are directly addressed is a social and practical safety feature we've developed over thousands of generations. It's going to take more than knowing Groucho isn't in the room with us to make us stop.

Direction of communication and the written word

On the surface of it, one might assume that writing can be either direct, such as in a comedic dating manual (in which the author is addressing the reader), or indirect, as in a narrative novel (in which the characters ignore your existence).

But the truth is, all prose is direct communication. The author tells you the story, imparts information to you.

It may seem like a contradiction that a written story is direct communication, while the same story acted out on stage is indirect. This is the difference, however, between comedy that is told and comedy that is shown. If I describe a scene to you, I'm communicating directly with you. If the same story is acted out by a cast, you'll be an observer.

So far, so good? Well here's the twist: prose is direct communication, but the receiver's role is passive.

We are actively engaged when watching a stand-up on video, even though we know he's not in the room with us. Our senses are stimulated by audio and visual cues that raise our attention level. The written word can't stimulate those senses. When we read, we're doing all the decoding and sensory reconstruction ourselves. We can't be fooled even subconsciously into believing that the author is with us.

[*Note*: This category is solely about the direction of communication in the immediate vehicle. The direction of communication for the joke itself (vehicular and non-vehicular) will be addressed when we get to enhancers and inhibitors. That's still a long way off, and I'll be honest: not all of you are going to survive the trip.]

2 Vicarious communication with other receivers

This refers to those vehicles in which we see or hear an audience reacting to the comedy. It may be that we're watching footage of a stand-up act that keeps cutting away to the audience, or we're simply watching a sitcom with a studio audience laugh-track. Unlike our earlier potential for communication with other receivers, these people are not in our reality, but they (or their reactions) are recorded in the vehicle itself.

An exercise in vehicle relativity

At first glance, it may be difficult to determine whether or not other receivers are part of the vehicle. As the great comedy detective Albert Einstein might say, it depends on where you stand.

Example: Receiver 1 is in the studio audience during a broadcast of *Saturday Night Live*. The vehicle he is watching is a live performance of a sketch. The reality of the vehicle does not include him—he is outside of the entertainment that is being presented (Figure 3.8):

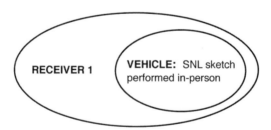

Receiver 1 is outside the vehicle

Receiver 2 watches the show as it is broadcast into his home. Rather than watching an in-person performance, he is watching a video. The video includes the laughter of an audience. The laughter is part of the soundtrack of the packaged entertainment and is therefore part of the vehicle. From his point of view, Receiver 1 is in the vehicle (Figure 3.9):

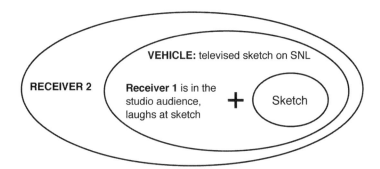

From the POV of Receiver 2, Receiver 1 is inside the vehicle

We've talked about the vehicle's language. (Technically, I talked about it. You looked out of the window.) Through years of conditioning, we understand the rules and the language of popular vehicles. It is understood by Receiver 2 that the studio audience are watching the show and that they are not part of the sketch. But they are still part of the vehicle. It is the nature of sitcoms or taped sketch shows that we entertain the dual reality of:

1   the dramatic conceit, and

2   the actuality that the drama is being performed for an audience.

It is the language of the vehicle.

How Vicarious Communication With Other Receivers Can Influence The Receiver

Much in the same way as we prick up our ears and pay a little extra attention when we're directly addressed by a projected image, we are also affected by the sight and sound of a projected audience.

Of course, we know we can't communicate with these people, but the sound of laughter—a uniquely human response—stirs some primal recognition within us. This is not to say we automatically laugh when we hear recorded laughter; however, the sound does have varying amounts of influence on receivers.

We have three levels of vicarious communication with other receivers:

1 *None*: Obviously, this refers to any vehicle with no recorded audience.

2 *Low level*: This brings us to our bad old laugh-track. Right up through the 1990s, networks insisted on slapping canned laughter onto comedies that were obviously not filmed in front of live audiences. Here are just a few: *The Andy Griffith Show, Gilligan's Island, Get Smart, The Munsters, The Addams Family, The Patty Duke Show, Mr. Ed, The Beverly Hillbillies, Green Acres, My Three Sons, The Monkees,* and the first few seasons of *M*A*S*H**.

   While it's true that these shows were created in a simpler time, the laugh-tracks on these shows did not always fool people. Sometimes they were added to footage where there was clearly no studio audience present, such as outdoor scenes, or in Bedrock on The Flintstones. Also, many laughs were used repeatedly from episode to episode and on multiple series, so they became familiar to the ear.

   Looking back, it's impossible to tell whether or not laugh-track engineers or network executives really thought they were fooling people, or if the laugh-track was simply a convention accepted by both providers and receivers: a stand-in audience to cue and influence people at home. Perhaps it was felt that the battle between logic and primal instinct was a no-brainer.

3 *High level:* This includes recorded or live/remote vehicles in which we can actually believe the laughs are genuine—whether they are or not.

With increased believability comes less conflict in the receiver's mind between logic and instinct.

ANECDOTE ALERT

Once, at *Frasier*, we shot half of an episode out on location, and showed the footage to a studio audience to record their laughter. The footage had a temp laugh-track thrown in by the editor just for this cut. When we showed it, the audience response was so huge that we had to re-cut the footage and put in long pauses to accommodate the protracted laughter from the audience.

Somehow, before the broadcast, the audience laughter got omitted and the temp laugh-track was put in by mistake. Of course, now the pauses were much longer than the laughs. The scenes were full of empty air. The show that the studio audience loved so much got slammed by the critics for being boring. Watching the exact same material with the actual laughter makes a huge difference.

Some people have strong feelings about laugh-tracks. They may bristle at the illogic of the more fake ones, or they may feel insulted by the idea that they need to be shown where the laughs are. They may also feel that the laugh-track is a form of cheating on the part of the producers or network, as a way of passing off something dull as something hilarious.

Even when the laughs are genuine, they can still harm enjoyment of the vehicle. I rarely watch David Letterman anymore. At the mildest joke the audience laughs and applauds, and the band plays a sting and another two minutes of my life go by. I find the laughter so out of proportion to the material that I can't watch it.

If you get a chance, watch the episode of *Ellen* in which she announces she's gay ("The Puppy Episode") and listen to that audience. In fact, listen to the audience from all the gay-themed episodes from about that time in the series. The response to every joke, even minor ones, is *huge*. The laughter is cathartic for the audience, which have very strong feelings about this character making this announcement on television. Their feelings reflect the beliefs of a group of people in Hollywood. Watching this show in a more conservative location, a receiver may be put off by the gay rally that seems to be going on in the bleachers.

Homework for the hardcore comedy detective

Once again, five receivers have encountered the same joke in different circumstances.

[*Note*: You may have to look up these vehicles to determine their direction of communication.]

1   *Receiver #1* finds the joke in the pages of this book.

	VEHICULAR COMEDY	
OUTER VEHICLES	type: **None** specific:	
IMMEDIATE VEHICLE	type: **Textbook** specific: **What Are You Laughing At?**	
DIRECTION OF COMMUNICATION	*direct* hybrid indirect	**RECEIVER ROLE:** active **passive** dual
VICARIOUS COMMUNICATION WITH OTHER RECEIVERS	*none* low high	

2   *Receiver #2* hears it in a recording of the Tom Lehrer song "Poisoning Pigeons in the Park," recorded with a live audience.

	VEHICULAR COMEDY	
OUTER VEHICLES	*type:* **None** *specific:*	
IMMEDIATE VEHICLE	*type:* **Song** *specific:* **Poisoning Pigeons In The Park**	
DIRECTION OF COMMUNICATION	*direct* *hybrid* *indirect*	**RECEIVER ROLE:** *active* *passive* *dual*
VICARIOUS COMMUNICATION WITH OTHER RECEIVERS	*none* *low* **high**	

3   *Receiver #3* comes across it in the movie *Alfie* (the original or the remake).

	VEHICULAR COMEDY	
OUTER VEHICLES	*type:* *specific:*	
IMMEDIATE VEHICLE	*type:* *specific:*	

DIRECTION OF COMMUNICATION	*direct*
	
	hybrid
	
	indirect
		RECEIVER ROLE: *active*
		
		               passive
		
		               dual

VICARIOUS COMMUNICATION WITH OTHER RECEIVERS	*none* *low* *high*	

4 *Receiver #4* sees that it comes from a witty description by Mark Twain in the pages of *Tom Sawyer*.

VEHICULAR COMEDY		
OUTER VEHICLES	type: specific:	
IMMEDIATE VEHICLE	type: specific:	

DIRECTION OF COMMUNICATION	direct
	hybrid
	indirect
		RECEIVER ROLE: active
		              passive
		              dual

VICARIOUS COMMUNICATION WITH OTHER RECEIVERS	none low high	

5   *Receiver #5 first sees it in a comic book; specifically, The Amazing Spider-Man.*

VEHICULAR COMEDY		
OUTER VEHICLES	*type:* *specific:*	
IMMEDIATE VEHICLE	*type:* *specific:*	

DIRECTION OF COMMUNICATION	*direct*
	
	hybrid
	
	indirect
		RECEIVER ROLE: *active*
		
		                passive
		
		                dual

VICARIOUS COMMUNICATION WITH OTHER RECEIVERS	*none* *low* *high*	

4

Level of control and identifying the source

4.1 LEVEL OF CONTROL

At this point we return to both vehicular and non-vehicular comedy. Having noted the device and the vehicle (if any), we can determine the level of control the receiver has during the comedic event.

What are levels of control?

1   *Receiver #1* is reading a book. He can put it down and walk away any time he wishes. The material will wait for him to return. He may go back and reread things, or skip ahead to another part.

2   *Receiver #2* is watching a play. If he misses something, the cast won't go back and do it again. He can't pause or skip ahead, and if he leaves, the comedy will go on and eventually finish without him.

Receiver #1 has a higher level of control over the event than Receiver #2.

The three levels

- *Low*: At a low level of control, the receiver cannot affect the rate at which he receives comedy. He cannot skip ahead or go back. At this level, the only control the receiver has is on or off, stay or go.

  We take in comedy at this level when we see plays, or films at the theater, or anything on TV that doesn't have any DVR functions. (This book is going to get a lot easier when TVs and computers finally merge.) It may also be true of bumper stickers or billboards, or any written word or still image content we can't control due to the circumstances in which we take in the information.

- *Medium*: When the receiver can pause, skip ahead and go backward, click to previous windows, etc., he has a mid-level of control.

  This occurs when we read books or take in pre-recorded audio and video on devices with these control functions.

- *High*: At this level, the receiver cannot only do some (if not all) of the above functions, he can also affect content.

  Some non-vehicular comedy, such as a humorous telephone conversation or Bob at work cutting up during the coffee break, affords us the opportunity to manipulate the very material by our own response or by whatever set-ups we throw to the source.

  Some vehicles, like video games or Mad Libs or improv, are built around this interactivity.

  However, this type of interactivity does not extend to websites in which user-submitted material is used. Once we submit our video to YouTube, it goes behind that invisible wall and is there for us to take in with only a medium level of control.

[*Note*: A device can have different levels of control. A laptop, for example, can bring you different media. If you use it to play a DVD, you have a mid-level of control. If you use it to play an interactive game or to video chat with a friend, you have a high level of control.]

How the level of control can influence the receiver

Higher control requires less commitment to the receiving process. If you know you can pause and go back to a TV show, you may be more likely to let down your level of concentration. You may be more likely to listen in on a conversation in the kitchen, or pay a little more attention to the pizza in front of you, or check your email, because if you miss something, you can always go back and pick it up again. Without the luxury of control, you are required to focus more on the comedy if you want to get the jokes and follow the story.

This happened to me recently when I spent a few weeks in a hotel and watched a TV that had no DVR features. After a few frustrating days of reflexively trying to reverse the content whenever I missed something, I found myself paying a little more attention to the screen.

Homework for the hardcore detective

In the following examples, five receivers encounter the same joke in different circumstances. If this takes you more than a minute, I have not done my job.

1   *RECEIVER #1* hears it in a phone conversation.

2   *RECEIVER #2* hears it on a comedy album downloaded from iTunes.

3   *RECEIVER #3* sees it in a feature film in a movie theater.

4   *RECEIVER #4* watches it on a TV show stored on his DVR.

5   *RECEIVER #5* reads it in a text conversation with a friend. (This is a tricky one: answer at the end.)

Answer

#5: In text conversations we can scroll back if we wish, as well as affect content by our responses. This indicates a high level of control.

4.2 IDENTIFYING THE SOURCE

In comedy, the source is the provider of the punchline. This is the person, animal, object, or cause-of-event that makes the receiver laugh. A more detailed description of the source's role will be presented as we begin dissecting jokes in the following sections.

Some sources are easy to identify. When Bob does something funny Bob is the source. But when Bob tells a joke about an elephant and a rabbit, and the rabbit has the punchline, is Bob the source, or is the rabbit? Likewise, when Groucho says something funny in a film, is he the source or is it the writers? Do we think of Lucy Ricardo as a source, or is it Lucille Ball?

When there are multiple sources there is generally one primary source and the rest are contributors. In this chapter we will learn how to distinguish between them. Understanding the difference is important in the study of comedy. As receivers, we pay special attention to the most prominent repre-sentative of the material. Our feelings for that entity will be a crucial factor in how we take in the joke.

How the identity of the source can influence the receiver

To put it simply, if your best friend tells you a joke, you may be more open to it than if the same joke is told by someone you hate.

When there are multiple sources, feelings for them can contradict each other. Back on *Cheers*, actor Kelsey Grammer had some highly publicized drug problems. Viewers could easily have felt one way about his character on the show and quite another about the actor playing the role.

ANECDOTE ALERT 1

Years ago I was lucky enough to meet George Burns, one of the iconic comedians of the twentieth century. At the time, he was well into his nineties. This was on a studio lot in Hollywood, and he asked me what I did there. I said, "I'm a writer." He puffed on his cigar and said, "So write something." I laughed heartily, as did all those who were present.

Some time later I realized that the line wasn't particularly funny. I just loved George Burns. His many years as one of my idols pretty much guaranteed that I was going to laugh at anything he said. This is an example of the dominant Type B laugh from Chapter 1.

ANECDOTE ALERT 2

Long ago, when I began doing stand-up comedy, I simply wrote jokes, grouped them by topic, went on stage on amateur night, and told them. I did well enough to keep coming back, but over time it became obvious that the act was weak in some way. One night I'd have a great set and the next time I'd bomb with the same material.

In my act I talked about my home life, politics, my girlfriend, sex, life at school, whatever. One day I glanced at a mirror and the answer suddenly came to me. Physically, I had always been young-looking. At the time I was 19 and I looked like I was still 15—the clean-cut boy next door who should have a paper route and call his father "Sir."

I realized that from the moment I was introduced by the emcee and I walked to the microphone, the audience was making assumptions about me based on my looks, the way I moved, the way I presented myself. When

I did more worldly material—sex and politics—I not only didn't have any credibility, but I was actively contradicting the audience's read of me.

I immediately threw out worldly material and added some new stuff that fit my appearance. Also, the next time I went on stage I adopted a nervous, enthusiastic energy combined with a little bit of wide-eyed innocence.

The effect was immediate and explosive. Suddenly, jokes that had only gotten mild laughs before got huge laughs. Within three weeks I started working professionally.

Before the change, my only function on stage was as a delivery system for the jokes. The act was something separate from myself. When I adopted the character, I literally joined with the material. Instead of just laughing at jokes, the audience was laughing at that guy on stage because he was funny. Every joke became another window into the character, reinforcing it.

The audience's feelings for my character greatly enhanced their openness to the material.

The primary source in non-vehicular comedy

The primary source is usually easy to identify in non-vehicular comedy: if Fred makes a funny observation, it's Fred. If Alicia writes you a funny email, it's Alicia. When Joe makes you do a knock-knock joke, or tells you the number of people screwing in a light bulb or pulls off some clever wordplay, or pretends to be your gay lover at the bowling alley, or puts fake vomit on your desk or does a scathing impression of you at parties, then it's Joe. Come to think of it, why do you still hang around with Joe?

In short, the source is the one who says or does something funny.

Earlier, Bob told a joke in which a rabbit has the punchline. The rabbit is not the source. The source must exist outside the joke.

But let's say your Uncle Tim tells you a funny story about his two-year-old daughter. Technically, the girl does exist in our reality, but she is not presenting you with comedy, having no part in its transmission. Uncle Tim is the teller, and as such he is the primary source.

	ELEMENTS OF COMEDIC EVENT	INFLUENCE ON RECEIVER
SOURCE	primary source: **Tim** relationship to receiver: **Uncle**	
CONTRIBUTING SOURCES	contributing sources and their relationship to the receiver:	

On the other hand, if Uncle Tim sends you a video of his daughter and you laugh, then the kid is the source and Uncle Tim is a contributing source; he has stepped aside from the limelight and let the kid do her own comedy.

	ELEMENTS OF COMEDIC EVENT	INFLUENCE ON RECEIVER
SOURCE	primary source: **Little kid** relationship to receiver: **Cousin**	
CONTRIBUTING SOURCES	contributing sources and their relationship to the receiver: **Tim - provider of video / Uncle**	

In each version, the primary source is the one from whom we most directly receive comedy.

In these examples, the sources are literally related to the receiver. The source may be a friend, a co-worker, or there may be no relationship at all.

The primary source in vehicular comedy

(Don't worry if this gets a little tricky. There's a nice chart at the end to keep it all straight.)

When Jerry Seinfeld does a monologue he is obviously the primary source, but what about when Lucy bakes a giant loaf of bread on *I Love Lucy*? Is Lucy Ricardo the primary source or is it Lucille Ball? What about the writers? The director? If Snoopy makes you laugh in the newspaper, is he the source or is Charles Schulz?

In these last two examples, fictional characters are the primary sources. We may admire the direction or the writing of the episode, as well as the talent of Lucille Ball, but the one baking the enormous loaf of bread is Lucy Ricardo. And indeed, this fictional character exists outside the joke; because we've engaged in this vehicle, we have agreed to Lucy's reality before the joke has come along. Our suspension of disbelief allows us to assign a level of reality to fictional characters that is separate from the actors playing them or the artists drawing them. Bugs Bunny, for example, can be a source.

The kid in the back has a question. What if we have a son who's in the school play and he has to wear a dress and we're laughing at him because we know how uncomfortable he is? Is the source the performer or the character?

In this case we are no longer laughing at the narrative. We've stepped outside of it to laugh at our son, who is now the primary source. (The kid in the back is not going to be a very nice parent.) The joke is also now non-vehicular.

Visible and invisible tellers

When comedy is communicated to us directly, we are being given the comedy by a teller. The teller can be visible (and immediately spotted as the source) or the teller can be invisible.

When Bill Cosby does his stand-up, he is the primary source of the comedy. He is visible to us as the teller, even as he launches into impressions of the people in his life.

When we read a novel, the teller is usually invisible, allowing his or her story to take center stage. This enables us to buy into the narrative and identify the characters as sources. As we read *The Hitchhiker's Guide to the Galaxy*, Arthur Dent's reality supersedes our knowledge that he is a creation of Douglas Adams.

But—

When Douglas Adams, in the role of narrator, gives us a funny description, he becomes visible, making himself the primary source. His description is outside the reality of Arthur Dent, who isn't aware that a funny description is being presented.

Likewise, in a sitcom or film, we often see jokes that are outside the knowledge of the character, such as a "cut-to" joke (where the character says, "This will be the best day of my life" and we cut to the character's house on fire). When the jokes come from how we tell the story rather than from the events in the story, then the source is the teller: the show or the film in question. If there is a "cut-to" joke on *Modern Family*, then the source is *Modern Family*.

Let's say you come across this creaky old joke in a magazine:

> A man walks into a restaurant and says to a hostess, "Do you serve crabs?"
> And the hostess says, "Sure, mister, we serve everyone! Come on in!"

We know the hostess cannot be the source: she exists solely within the joke. So we assign the role to the teller which would be the magazine itself, or perhaps to the editor who collected the jokes.

Stand-alone jokes that are shown

As we know, Snoopy, a recurring character, can be a source. When we encounter a single panel cartoon that does not make use of any recurring character, we consider the teller to be the source. We think, "a Gahan Wilson cartoon" or "a

New Yorker cartoon." The source for any joke in *The Far Side* (non-recurring characters) is Gary Larsen.

When stand-alone jokes are performed for us, say, as black-out sketches (sketches that dramatize a single joke), we tend to credit the actors as the primary sources. This is because black-outs are usually parts of a larger overall vehicle (a sketch comedy show) in which the cast members have made themselves known to the audience. These people existed in the vehicle prior to the joke—their real identity overshadows the characters they play. This holds true with improv. Since the entertainment value of improv is focused on the creation of comedy as much (if not more) than the comedy itself, it is imperative that we keep the actors' true identities in our minds at all times.

This chart provides is a handy checklist for identifying the primary source in vehicular comedy:

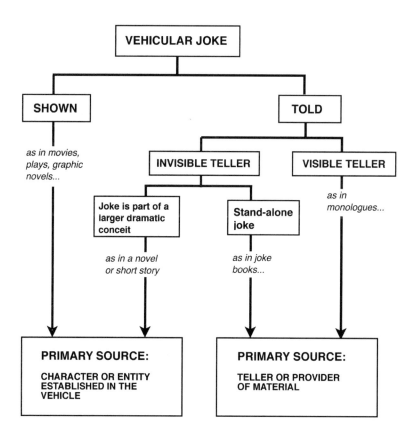

Contributing sources

Now that we've decided Lucy Ricardo is the primary source, we're still left with Lucille Ball, as well as the writers and the director. They are the contributing sources, as are the producers, prop people, wardrobe designers, electricians, editors, and anyone who had anything to do with the creation and presentation of the vehicle. How many of these are pertinent to the comedic experience? Only the ones of which the receiver is aware.

In the case of *I Love Lucy*, Lucille Ball is the contributing source for whom most people will have pre-existing feelings. These feelings will color their openness to taking in comedy in which her character is the primary source.

Sometimes a receiver may have a personal connection with some lower tier contributor and the association will affect the experience. I know a woman whose son was in charge of answering phones in the production offices of a sitcom. She often referred to the series as "my son's show." Her pride made her watch it more appreciatively. Likewise, if some guy you hated in college had some incidental role in the creation of a huge film, you may watch it more critically than if you had no connection to it at all.

Homework for the hardcore comedy detective

In the following examples, differentiate between primary and contributing sources. Unless specifically noted, assume that the receiver has no relationship to any of the people mentioned.

1   *Example #1.* A Charles Addams cartoon, brought to your attention by John, your roommate.

	ELEMENTS OF COMEDIC EVENT	INFLUENCE ON RECEIVER
SOURCE	*primary source:* **Charled Addams** *relationship to receiver:* **None**	
CONTRIBUTING SOURCES	*contributing sources and their relationship to the receiver:* **John / roommate**	

2   *Example #2.* In an episode of *Modern Family*, Phil Dunphy (played by Ty Burrell) does something funny.

	ELEMENTS OF COMEDIC EVENT	INFLUENCE ON RECEIVER
SOURCE	*primary source:* **Phil Dunphy** *relationship to receiver:* **None**	
CONTRIBUTING SOURCES	*contributing sources and their relationship to the receiver:* **Ty Burrell / none**	

3   *Example #3.* Ty Burrell describes the same scene on a talk show.

	ELEMENTS OF COMEDIC EVENT	INFLUENCE ON RECEIVER
SOURCE	primary source: relationship to receiver:	
CONTRIBUTING SOURCES	contributing sources and their relationship to the receiver:	

4   *Example #4.* Bill Cosby acts out a joke in which his brother, Russell, has the punchline.

	ELEMENTS OF COMEDIC EVENT	INFLUENCE ON RECEIVER
SOURCE	primary source: relationship to receiver:	
CONTRIBUTING SOURCES	contributing sources and their relationship to the receiver:	

5   *Example #5.* Ventriloquist Jeff Dunham is insulted by his dummy
    Walter (answer at the end).

	ELEMENTS OF COMEDIC EVENT	INFLUENCE ON RECEIVER
SOURCE	*primary source:* *relationship to receiver:*	
CONTRIBUTING SOURCES	*contributing sources and their relationship to the receiver:*	

Answer

#5: The primary source is Walter. We buy into a dramatic conceit, agreeing
to the reality of the dummy before any individual jokes come along. This is
different than when Bill Cosby takes on the character of his brother. There is
never a time when we're forced to pretend that he and Cosby are sharing the
stage.

PART TWO

COMEDIC INFORMATION

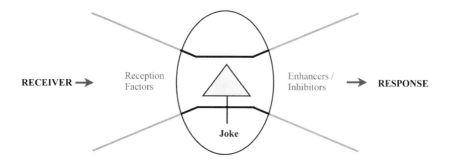

In this section we look at comedic information, or the joke. We take it apart and examine the core variables that exist in all comedy. We also see how the interplay between these variables affects response, how jokes grow old, and how they eventually die.

5

Fundamental components

5.1 THE RECEIVER'S BRAIN: HARD-WIRED FOR COMEDY?

We all live our lives with a big rule book in our head. It tells us how the world and its creatures should behave. We build this rule book ourselves, based on years of learning and experience.

We build these rule books while we're young, taking in, measuring, and defining every piece of information put in front of us. This engages us with the world, forcing us to constantly ask what and why and how. Millions of mental and tactile impressions must be cataloged. It is an enormous task, and it's how we develop a sense of possibility and probability.

As adults, however, we interact with the world differently, because we have our rule books in place. Rather than defining, our primary mode of processing is comparing/projecting. We instantly and automatically compare incoming information to our libraries, checking to see if everything falls within a normative range. If it does, we can dispense with it easily and go into routine patterns of behavior. When we aren't cataloging every minute, days slip from our memories and thus our experience of time. This may account for why time crawls in childhood but zips by during adulthood.

Every piece of information has numerous connections to other pieces of information. For example, when I say "car" your first tier of associations is right there at the ready. They might include cars you've driven, car trivia, famous cars, car construction, car references, like half the Beach Boys catalogue, automobile history, etc. These associations may be sensory—you may recall the smell of a new car, the feeling of carsickness, the sound of the turn signal, rain against the windshield. Then there's car paraphernalia: garages, car washes, streets, traffic laws. You also have associations about the word itself: that it rhymes with "jar," it's the first part of "cartoon," etc.

The connections get increasingly tenuous, but remember that each of the associations has its own associations. Without breaking a sweat, your brain can take you from "car" to "Ford," to "Presidents" which includes "Lincoln" which is a "car." Of such connections, jokes are made.

Two facets of our cognitive nature are integral to the existence of comedy:

1   Our automatic comparison/projection mode. When something appears on our radar that is beyond the range of normal, it draws our attention. We are hard-wired to be on the look-out for incongruity.

2   Mental referencing and cross-referencing of information. A good comedian or comedy writer understands how to take advantage of and manipulate the way in which our brains make connections.

5.2 COMEDIC INFORMATION: THE TRIANGLE

All comedic information can be broken down into a few basic components. Unlike possible reception factors and enhancers/inhibitors, these core components exist in every comedic experience.

We start with the receiver, the set-up, and the source (Figure 5.1):

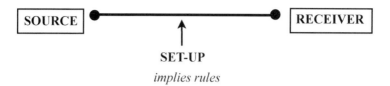

SET-UP

implies rules

The set-up is information that implies rules in the mind of the receiver. These are the rules—not always overtly stated—against which the incongruity of the finished joke will be measured. Rules may come from our mental rule books, or they may be new rules, created as part of the internal logic of the joke or comedic vehicle. We will discuss implied rules in more depth in Chapter 6.

Origin of the set-up

The set-up may be provided by the source, as in a self-contained joke. A set-up can be "A guy walks into a bar," or any premise to which he can attach a punchline. This also extends to physical comedy. A performer may set himself up by establishing a pattern of behavior (Figure 5.2):

S ⎯⎯⎯⎯⎯⎯⎯⟶ R

A guy walks into a bar...

The receiver may also set up the joke. Some years ago I was having lunch with writer David Lloyd. The lunch included a basket of different-sized bread rolls. I asked him if there were any small rolls, and without missing a beat he said, "No, only small actors." I, as the receiver, had provided the set-up, as represented by the arrow in (Figure 5.3):

S ⟵⎯⎯⎯⎯⎯⎯⎯ R

Are there any small rolls?

The set-up may also come from a third party. If I, the receiver, watch a conversation between Abbott and Costello, a set-up can come from Abbott, which will then be paid off by the source, Costello (Figure 5.4):

The source and the punchline

The one thing that must always be done by the source is to provide the second piece of information, which we will shorthand as the punchline.

A source can be a performer. It may also be anyone who does something inadvertently funny. Nature or happenstance can be the source, as can a fictional character. The source can create the punchline without any knowledge of doing so. The receiver and the source may be one and the same—have you ever had a thought occur to you that made you laugh?

Using the last three examples, we will place the punchlines as they originate from the source at a 45-degree angle from the set-up (Figure 5.5):

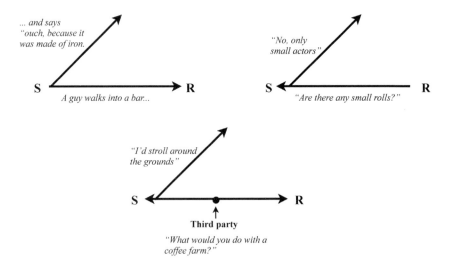

The receiver's job: cognitive process

Having now received two pieces of information, the receiver must mentally connect the set-up to the punchline in order to assemble the finished concept. The finished triangle represents a completed joke (Figure 5.6):

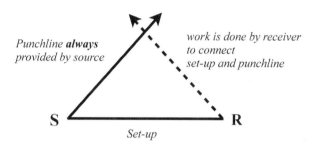

*Punchline **always** provided by source*

work is done by receiver to connect set-up and punchline

S   R

Set-up

It's common to think of the joke in terms of a one-two punch: the set-up starts it off and the punchline finishes the job. As we'll see, humor can also be constructed in such a way that the punchline is the first element given to the receiver, triggering the awareness of an unexpressed set-up. A punchline can also be embedded in the language of the set-up.

The triggered set-up

We are often confronted by funny things with no apparent set-up. When that happens, where do the rules come from?

They are triggered by the punchline.

This is easily done when the set-up is reality itself. We live in the set-up, so it doesn't always need to be openly stated. It is assumed that the receiver has some passing familiarity with it.

Here's the joke: you feed a baby a pickle, and the baby makes a very funny face.

On the surface, it would seem that feeding the baby the pickle might be the set-up. After all, haven't we always heard that the set-up precedes the punchline?

The pickle, however, is merely a stimulus. The true set-up is triggered retro-actively by the punchline. The set-up is in your knowledge of the baby's usual array of expressions (Figure 5.7):

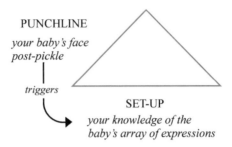

The incongruous expression is compared and contrasted with the baby's normal range of expressions. The event is enhanced by your feelings for the child, safe sadism, and identification. The face may remind you of a family member or someone famous, giving you another layer to the joke.

Misfires

Figures 5.8 to 5.11 represent comedy misfires—too much or too little infor-mation in the joke, or insufficient cognitive process.

For example, if I make a joke about Noam Chomsky, and the receiver doesn't know who that is, the joke may fall flat (Figure 5.8):

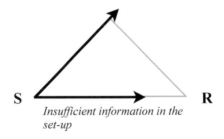

Likewise, a punchline may omit integral information, or reference an element that is unknown to the receiver (Figure 5.9):

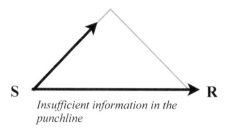

Insufficient information in the punchline

Sometimes the receiver just can't put it all together (Figure 5.10):

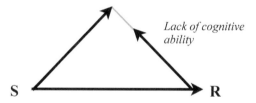

Lack of cognitive ability

The source can also give away too much information in the punchline, subtracting from the amount of work required by the receiver (Figure 5.11):

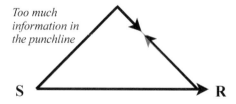

Too much information in the punchline

This results in a completed but ultimately unsatisfying joke.

5.3 THE CORE VARIABLES

Cognitive process and incongruity

In order to assemble the triangle, some amount of cognitive process is required by the receiver. Some jokes may be presented with all the pieces laid out for the receiver, while others need to be figured out, or solved, through logic.

When the triangle is solved, it will present a picture containing some degree (or multiple degrees) of incongruity.

Thus, cognitive process and incongruity are the two core variables in every comedic experience. The interaction of these two elements is the key to the joke. You may remember from Chapter 1 that the two indicators for comedic potential are visceral (recognition of incongruity) and cognitive/social (recognition of play). Well, here's where it all happens.

Let's use this old Groucho Marx joke:

I once shot an elephant in my pajamas. How he got in my pajamas, I don't know.

If you've never heard this joke you'll have to solve the logic of it in order to realize that the elephant is wearing pajamas. Only by doing the math, as it were, will you find the incongruity (Figure 5.12):

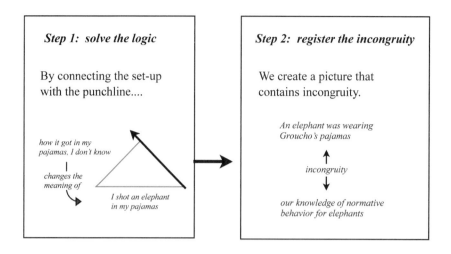

Once the comedic idea is assembled, we are free to experience the attendant enhancers/inhibitors that come bubbling up as our psyches are confronted with the incongruous picture. There are different levels of incongruity, and there are different degrees of cognitive process playing against each other throughout all comedy.

Sharp-eyed theorists will recognize that this approach (using logic to assemble a picture in order to find incongruity) is kind of the inverse of *incongruity resolution theory*. This theory says that we detect incongruity and then resolve it. I believe that the joy of comedy is in assembling an idea that contains and maintains incongruity.

Angles of incongruity and cognitive process

Angles of incongruity

As we'll discuss in the following section, some combinations are more incongruent than others. We will be creating approximate benchmarks for measuring incongruity. These measurements will appear in the triangle shown in (Figure 5.13):

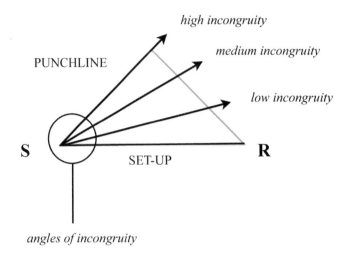

angles of incongruity

[*Note*: Understand that the punchline is not necessarily incongruous to the set-up. The angle of incongruity is based on the incongruity found in the completed joke, as they are measured against rules that have been inferred from the set-up.]

Angles of cognitive process

All comedy requires some degree of cognitive processing on the part of the receiver to assemble the finished idea. Clearly, not all jokes are created equal; some require more work than others.

We'll explore three cognitive benchmarks for comedy processing in Chapter 7. They appear in the triangle in (Figure 5.14):

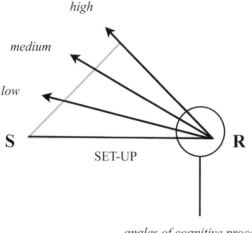

high

medium

low

S

SET-UP

R

angles of cognitive process

The line of cognitive process represents the work done by the receiver to combine the set-up and the punchline, resulting in the creation of the incongruous image.

Combining the elements

Once we've put our measurements in place for incongruity and cognitive process, we can examine any joke, any comedic incident, and find its approximate location in the comedy landscape. These triangles show us the dance between the jolt of incongruity and the cognitive thrill of problem solving.

Combinations of the two angles will be represented as in the following examples:

1 A joke with high incongruity, low level of cognitive processing (Figure 5.15):

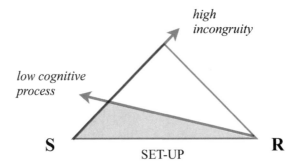

2   A joke with medium incongruity, medium cognitive process (Figure 5.16):

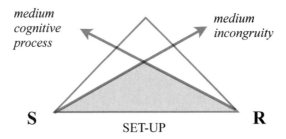

With three demarcations for both incongruity and cognitive process, we have nine benchmarks for comedic information and assembly. This does not imply that there are only nine jokes in the universe.

Our ability to compare, contrast, and juxtapose concepts enables us to fit an endless variety of content onto the triangle without obvious exposure to the structures beneath. We can juxtapose the manner in which information is transmitted in limitless ways. Keep in mind also that there are a multitude of possible enhancers to any joke. (Many of them are so overpowering as to lead receivers—and researchers—to believe that the enhancer *is* the joke.) Every piece of data we take in may bring up feelings or associations or memories that in turn bring up feelings. And we have yet to explore the many aspects of awareness that color our experience of comedy. With all of this going on in infinite combination and degree, these basic triangles can stay hidden indefinitely.

Warnings for the comedy detective

You are now entering the trickiest part of comedy dissection. Here are a few points that will be repeated during following sections because they can't be stressed enough.

The combined levels of incongruity and cognitive process are in no way measurements of the "funniness" of a joke. While we will be finding patterns among various triangles (comedy that is appreciated as clever vs. comedy that is viscerally amusing), any triangle can be highly effective. Even the smallest one can get huge laughs. Take Bill Cosby. He can talk about his family in such a way that it takes no large amount of cognitive processing to understand it, and the behavior he describes may only contain low levels of incongruity. Yet the huge enhancers of identification, nostalgia, and appreciation for Cosby's performance can make for a hilarious experience. Knowledge and manipulation of enhancers are powerful tools in the arsenal of writers and performers.

When estimating angles for comedy, we must wear our logic hats. Not all comedy will be easy to identify, for a number of reasons:

1   There are so many enhancers/inhibitors at work that it takes some practice to eliminate them from our view of the joke. In order to establish the nature of the triangle being analyzed, it must be laid bare so that we can work dispassionately with the structure.

2   Each succeeding level of cognitive processing can make use of elements from the previous levels. Because of this, we may notice characteristics and shout: "Medium cognitive process!" without

realizing that these characteristics are being used in conjunction with higher level ones to create a more complicated joke.

3   There will be a temptation to identify styles of comedy and try to assign them angles of incongruity and cognitive process wholesale, like saying that all slapstick has low-angle cognitive process and high-angle incongruity, or that all wordplay has a certain angle of this and a certain angle of that. Every style of humor has many variations as far as the individual jokes go; otherwise they'd get very repetitive. In other words, every joke has to be examined on its own.

Ultimately, it's a good thing for comedy that this type of dissection and identification can be difficult, because it means that comedy isn't always transparent. If it were, we would start seeing through the jokes too quickly, damaging our enjoyment of it.

6

Incongruity

6.1 INCONGRUITY

Incongruity is the chasm created by the overlay of two concepts as we understand them. The joining of these ideas may result in a disharmony or unexpected conceptual hybrid. "Concepts" can be narrative events, physical objects, musical strains, behaviors, whatever we wish.

Does this mean we can randomly slap ideas together and expect to get laughs? Does it mean we can get bigger laughs by combining things that are increasingly dissimilar? Of course not—remember how I totally schooled Schopenhauer in the overview?

Even incongruity has laws, as far as comedy goes. Clearly, a combination has to be incongruous enough to get our attention if it is to stand out against the common and expected incongruities of day-to-day existence. And yet we can't go too far. Take the type of wordplay in which one word is substituted for another. The substitute word needs to be both similar and different to the word it's replaced. Without similarities the words can't be played against each other, and without differences there'd be no point. This is why, in Mad Libs, they have to tell you the kinds of words to fill in. Pure randomness is too unreliable for sustained comedy.

This law remains intact, even when it comes to meta-comedy—shows and sketches and drawings that make us laugh because they're not funny, shows that seem to be incongruous only for the sake of incongruity itself. Meta-comedy can only work if it is presented in a way that is similar in shape to that which we are accustomed to seeing as funny. They use referential markers to remind us of the form being subverted, which forces us to pull up the rule book for comedy itself.

That is, we use comedy to make fun of comedy by not being funny, which makes it funny.

Incongruous to what?

It is often said that in comedy, the punchline provides information that is incongruous to the set-up. This is only partly true. We can state it more accurately this way:

The receiver combines the set-up and the punchline to create an idea that is incongruous to *rules inferred from the set-up*:

set-up combined with punchline

↑

incongruity

↓

rules inferred from the set-up

First, we assemble the incongruous image by combining the set-up with the punchline. The finished idea will be incongruous to rules that have been called into play by the set-up.

Example:

Set-up: Your mama's so fat ...
Punchline: that when she rolls over, the tides change.

Notice that, strictly speaking, the punchline is not incongruous to the stated set-up. If anything, the punchline builds on the premise.

To find the incongruity, we must first combine set-up and punchline. When we do, we are led to create a picture of someone so large that her gravitational pull exerts pressure on our oceans. This makes her approximately the size of the moon. What is this incongruous to? Let's go back and find the rules that can be inferred from the set-up.

The subject is "your mama." This is not literally the receiver's mother, of course. This form of joke is commonly told by people who have not actually met your mother, so "your mama" is just a generic fill-in person.

Since we have not been told otherwise, the universe in the set-up is our own. This means we are working from a well-known bell-curve for human heights and weights. These are the rules inferred from the set-up, and here we find an important fact:

Unless we are specifically told otherwise, the default universe in comedy is reality.

In other words, the rule book of norms we build in the first part of our lives is the set-up we carry around with us. (In a narrative vehicle, the default set-up comes from the rules of reality as established in the vehicle.)

So between the real world and the notion of Mama being the size of the moon, we find the incongruity (Figure 6.1):

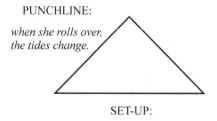

PUNCHLINE:

when she rolls over,
the tides change.

SET-UP:

Your mama's so fat --

INFERRED RULE:

joke uses rule book for our world,
with normative measures for human
heights and weights

When we see a hat blow off a man's head and onto the head of a statue, we immediately compare the event to our rule book of normalcy and recognize incongruity, based on its odds of occurrence (Figure 6.2):

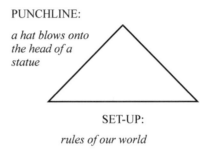

PUNCHLINE:

a hat blows onto the head of a statue

SET-UP:

rules of our world

Inferred rules of transmission

Inferred rules are not merely about the joke's content. The way the set-up is communicated will imply rules about the type of language that is to be used, the source's attitude, even the speed and rhythm of communication, any one of which can be broken by the punchline. If you suddenly SCREAM the last word of a sentence, you will thwart an expectation based on how you said everything leading up to the last word.

Creating incongruity

Much comedy begins with the simple words, "what if" or "can you imagine if," or "wouldn't it be funny if." These words imply "what if, *in our reality.* ..." This gives us the rule book of reality to work from. The punchline will then give us an incongruous concept (Figure 6.3):

PUNCHLINE:

*My dog suddenly
started singing
opera?*

SET-UP:

Wouldn't it be funny if (in our reality)--

We project comedic outcomes all the time without actually saying "what if." A group of employees watch as the boss tries to act cool around a good-looking client. An employee says, "Watch he throws up on her coat ..." or even just "He throws up on her coat. ..." We understand the shorthand.

Compare this to a line from the late George Carlin:

If a cow laughed, would milk shoot out her nose?

Here, the incongruity of the laughing cow is acknowledged in the set-up. We are asked to accept the idea—temporarily add it to our rule book—in order to get to a further incongruous idea.

When is a talking fish normal?

As soon as a fantasy element is introduced into the set-up, we adjust our rule book to include whatever rules we know about the fantasy, and this becomes the point from which we measure incongruity. When a joke begins with "Superman is flying around Metropolis ..." we pull out the Superman rule book and we're ready for the joke. In that universe, it is not incongruous for Superman to fly. When watching a Bugs Bunny cartoon, we work from the Bugs Bunny rule book, so it is not incongruous when he talks.

From the point of view of reality, it is, of course, incongruous for a rabbit to speak or for a humanoid to fly, and if we wish to step back and enjoy those incongruities we are welcome to do so. But it is understood that this is not the point of the joke.

Let's take a joke in which a talking fish is not incongruous. First, the joke announces itself as a joke. It's told in the present tense, establishing two fish as the protagonists. This is basic joke language, with which we are usually familiar. The rules of talking animals and mythical characters are called into play, and we are not surprised when the fish speak. We are, however, surprised to find them in a military tank. This is new, and not covered in the rule book. In fact, the fish themselves seem a little unnerved by the situation (Figure 6.4):

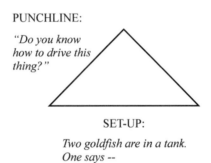

PUNCHLINE:

"Do you know how to drive this thing?"

SET-UP:

Two goldfish are in a tank.
One says --

To show just how easily we accept the idea of talking fish, let's remove the humor. If you tell this version of the joke, you will only get a blank look (unless you are telling the joke ironically or unless the receiver laughs at your feeble attempt at humor). We still have a talking fish, but that's been established in the set-up, so it's not seen as incongruous in and of itself. The fish has to say something that leads to an unexpected incongruity (Figure 6.5):

PUNCHLINE:

"Good morning"

SET-UP:

Two goldfish are in a tank.
One says --

Changes in the rule book

As we'll discuss when we get to comedic entropy, rules do change. Back in the 1960s, *Mr. Ed* was a TV series about a talking horse. The first time Ed—the horse—spoke, it was very incongruous. As the audience accepted this impossibility the rule changed: a talking horse was possible in the Mr. Ed universe. From that point, the dominant incongruity had to be found in what the horse was saying, rather than in the simple fact that he was talking. The talking became part of the set-up; a secondary incongruity that supported the jokes, but didn't have to be enjoyed every time out.

Relative incongruity

Imagine two people watching a clip from *Mr. Ed*. One receiver has seen the show before; one hasn't. In the clip, Ed makes a joke. Each receiver works from a different rule book. For the receiver who knows the series, the dominant incongruity is in what Ed says. For the other, the dominant incongruity may be the talking horse, combined with the incongruity contained in his joke:

RECEIVER 1 (familiar with *Mr. Ed*):

Dominant incongruity: Content of Mr. Ed's joke

Secondary Incongruity: Mr. Ed is a talking horse.

RECEIVER 2 (not familiar with *Mr. Ed*):

Dominant Incongruity: Mr. Ed is a talking horse.

Secondary incongruity: Content of Mr. Ed's joke

Differences in receiver rule books can lead to different perceptions of incongruity. To me, ants covered in chocolate may be an incongruous combination, but not to someone who has been raised on them. Likewise, the idea of cops randomly beating someone may seem hugely incongruous in some neighborhoods, but like an average day in the inner city.

Multiple incongruities

Perhaps by now you've realized that a joke can have several incongruities.

The number of incongruities experienced in any joke depends on the receiver. Some will simply recognize the primary incongruity and move on, while others may turn the joke over in their heads and enjoy more than one level.

Often, additional incongruities are mentally provided by the receiver. A joke may be like a stone thrown into a pond, creating ripples of incongruity in the mind. When I tell a joke about your mama being big enough to use Mexico as a tanning bed, how many incongruous elements will you string together in your head? Everyone's mental picture is different. Will "your" mama crush people and buildings? What is she wearing? An enormous bathing suit? Giant sunglasses? Is she covered in tons and tons of suntan lotion? Is she on the news? Does she swat helicopters like she would mosquitoes? What's her attitude? It would be interesting to see if differences in mental picturing are indicative of differences in senses of humor.

From dominant to secondary incongruity

Most of us have enjoyed social situations in which incongruities are strung together spontaneously by a group. First, someone throws out some incongruous idea, like the woman using Mexico to suntan herself. Now that this incongruity has been established (like Carlin's laughing cow), we can climb the incongruity ladder. Someone else tosses in something about planes being used to dump lotion on her, which may then lurch into a tangent about the villages around her perimeter, and which ones are more desirable to live in than others This may inspire someone to take on the role of a realtor, trying to persuade a couple to buy a home in one of the more questionable areas, spinning the negatives into positives. Much bodily function humor here. This can go on for what seems like hours, and get increasingly absurd. This type of interaction is socially bonding and can be hilarious in the moment.

In this instance, the comedic run radiates from the premise of a woman-as-large-as-a-country, which starts out as the dominant incongruity in the first joke, and then moves off to be the set-up—and secondary incongruity—in all the other jokes. Like Mr. Ed's talking, the initial incongruity recedes as the rule takes hold.

Visually based comedy

Although all the examples in this section have been language-based, the rules hold true with visual humor.

Sometimes in slapstick, we see people abusing each other without any clear set-up in the context. The Three Stooges whacked each other around all the time. Why is this funny? Where is the set-up against which the slapstick can be called a punchline?

The set-up is normative behavior as established in the context of the joke. The world of the Three Stooges is supposed to roughly mirror our own. We are supposed to identify it as familiar so that we can use our standard behavioral assumptions (for people and physics) from the same rule book we use in our real lives. Against this "normality," the behavior of the Stooges is incongruous.

It has often been pointed out that there was a basic conceptual error in making the Marx Brothers film *At The Circus*. The Marx Brothers were zany characters—putting them against a background that was also zany diminished their incongruity. They fared better in *A Night At The Opera*, where their very existence amidst a world of highbrow stuffed shirts created incongruity.

Incongruity resolution and why it doesn't work

Incongruity resolution is a theory that presents a two-part process for how we take in comedy:

1   First, we detect incongruity.

2   Then we resolve it.

For example, we have this line:

"Take my wife—please!"

According to incongruity resolution, our first step is to see that the word "please" is somehow incongruous to the set-up. Then we are forced to go back and change our meaning of the words in the set-up so that the punchline makes logical sense. That's the resolution part. Then we all laugh and clap each other on the back. I added that part sarcastically.

Another example:

A man is driving on the freeway when he gets a call from his anxious wife. She says, "Honey, be careful! There's a report on the news that a man is driving the wrong way on the freeway!" "One man?" says the husband, "There are hundreds of them!"

Again, we find unexpected words in the punchline: "There are hundreds of them!" This is supposed to be the incongruity. Now, we are forced to go back and realize that the man was driving the wrong way. That's the resolution.

There are problems with incongruity resolution. First, it's based on the flawed equation:

$$incongruity = \frac{b\ (punchline)}{a\ (set\text{-}up)}$$

That is to say that the theory forces us to always think of the punchline as incongruous to the set-up. This is supposedly the sole incongruity of the joke.

As we've discussed, the true formula for comedic incongruity is:

$$incongruity = \frac{a \text{ } (set\text{-}up) + b \text{ } (punchline)}{rules \text{ } inferred \text{ } from \text{ } a \text{ } (set\text{-}up)}$$

Using this equation, we can put the funny back into the joke. Go back to:

"Take my wife—please!"

Incongruity resolution says that the word "please" is incongruous because it is unexpected. But this is simply not so.

Every day, linguistic pressure from unexpected words causes us to go back and shift meanings in our heads. You may be hearing a story about someone called Terry and assume that Terry is a man until the speaker happens to say "she." Quickly, you go back and overlay the new information and make the correction. This is not a function of comedic structure—it is a function of our language structure. And because we understand this and allow for it, the unexpected words are not incongruous. In short, incongruity resolution looks for incongruity in the wrong place.

When we encounter the word "please" we automatically go back and resolve the logic of the entire sentence. Again, we don't resolve the incongruity. We resolve the logic.

When the logic is resolved, we find we have co-created an incongruous picture of a man begging us to take away his wife. (This image may be enhanced by our feelings for the performer, appreciation of delivery, identification, familiarity, or aggression. It may also be inhibited by any of these.)

It's the finished picture that gives us the joke's incongruity. Our appreciation may be enhanced by the brief cognitive thrill of having solved the logic.

Let's return to the guy driving the wrong way on the freeway. When we hit the punchline "There are hundreds of them" the unexpected words do not signal incongruity (again, because we allow for the possibility of unexpected, meaning-shifting words). Instead, the unexpected words cause us to resolve the logic of the sentence (step 1) in order to construct and identify an incongruous picture (step 2).

Look at the difference:

In incongruity resolution, the incongruity in the joke is the identification of unexpected words "there are hundreds of them." In reality, however, the incongruity is in the *finished* picture. We find a man driving the wrong way on the freeway, too dumb to know what he's doing. We may enjoy the idea of this guy blindly causing cars to swerve around, horns honking, causing all kinds of havoc, while innocently talking to his wife. This is the incongruity! This is the funny! And it gets lost in incongruity resolution.

The goal of comedy is to create and maintain incongruity for as long as possible, not resolve it away.

Homework for the hardcore comedy detective

As you observe and experience comedy, see if you can:

1 Identify the inferred rules that are used to launch incongruity.

2 Find more than one incongruity in any joke.

3 Notice where the laugh lives in relation to the joke; that is, if we're laughing primarily because of the content (internal), or because of the circumstances surrounding the joke (external), or both.

6.2 ESTIMATING LEVELS OF INCONGRUITY

It's safe to say that some combinations are more incongruous than others:

- Pancakes and syrup are not an incongruous combination.

- Pancakes and ketchup are more incongruous.

- Pancakes and motor oil even more so.

- Pancakes and the femur of former First Lady Bess Truman even more so.

A simple list like this makes it easy to see how ideas can be increasingly incongruous when juxtaposed against the rules of a set-up. Yet the task of quantifying incongruity isn't an exact one. It's rather like determining when a hill becomes a mountain. The best we can do is identify basic conceptual signposts that are both distinct enough and broad enough to make effective groupings.

Our next diagram shows angles of incongruity. These lines represent the incongruity in the finished joke: the set-up plus the punchline will determine the angle of incongruity. Again, it is not meant to suggest that the punchline is incongruous to the set-up (Figure 6.6):

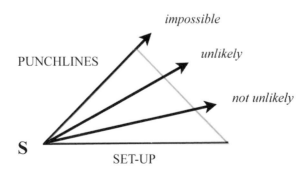

The levels are based on estimated odds of occurrence in nature (meaning, of course, the nature established in the set-up). If an incident occurs frequently in our world, like rain falling from the sky, it has a low level of incongruity; it is not an unlikely occurrence. If an incident occurs very rarely, like a meteor falling on your house, there would be a higher level of incongruity, based on the unlikelihood of the event. Finally, we have zero odds, like when I know it's raining because my dog called me and told me so.

Gray areas: keeping it fluid

At what point does an event or a conceptual idea go from "not unlikely" to "unlikely?" Or from "unlikely" to "impossible?" We know off the top of our heads that seeing a six-foot, nine-inch person in our lives is not unlikely. If we start adding inches to him, though, at what height does he become a rarity? And what is a rarity? Does it mean that people in his height bracket are one person in a hundred? A thousand? Obviously we can't be exact. We can only count on the relative likelihood of our bumping into this person among the eight billion other people we have to worry about from day to day.

Likewise, when does unlikely become impossible? It is technically possible that every physically able man, woman, and child in Kentucky can jump in the air at the same time, but overcoming the logistics makes the event so improbable that, by practical definition, it becomes impossible. Beyond that, there are clearly degrees of impossibility, such as the difference between a thousand-story building and a million-story building, but charting the impossible is not on our to-do list today, thank you.

Understand that we cannot expect to find precision here. We can only estimate levels of incongruity, based on the information in our rule books. Although there will always be room for overlap and disagreement, the incongruity level of most comedy can be estimated fairly easily.

[Note: Throughout this text, there will be shorthand references to the angles of incongruity as high, medium, and low. Keep in mind that when we talk about medium incongruity, we're still referring to the highest level of incongruity that can be achieved without breaking the reality established in the set-up. In our diagram, the angles of incongruity are evenly spaced, but this is for graphic simplicity; we are not literally dividing incongruity into thirds.]

Taking a concept through increasing levels of incongruity

In this exercise, we'll use a familiar joke set-up to familiarize ourselves with the three angles of incongruity and how they apply to basic concepts.

"Your mama's so fat …"

Okay, we have a fat woman here. Rather than actually putting in punchlines, let's take some stabs at incongruity:

1   Your mama's as fat as someone who weighs 400 pounds.

2   Your mama's as fat as the fattest person in the world.

3   Your mama's as fat as a cow.

4   Your mama's as fat as a city.

5   Your mama's as fat as the world.

6   Your mama's as fat as the universe.

7   Your mama's as fat as ten universes.

8   Your mama's as fat as a hundred universes.

9   Your mama's as fat as glibbity globbity.

Obviously, by the time we reach number nine, the search for maximum incongruity has led us off the map of comprehension. Tossing that one aside, we'll try grouping the others by their level of incongruity.

The first step is to understand which rules have been established as our starting point. Since we have not been told otherwise, we are working from the rule book of our own reality. Based on those rules, how incongruous are the eight choices above?

- *Angle one: Low incongruity/not unlikely* (Figure 6.7):

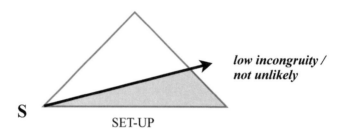

Notice the wording in this category: "not unlikely." Why not just "likely?"

It's because we're working with a wide range of possibilities. If we were to use the word "likely," it would appear that we are referring to circumstances that have anywhere from, say, 50% to 100% probability of existence.

But we want to include circumstances with probability levels even as low as 5% or 10%. It is not likely that an event with a 5% level of probability will occur, but it is not so crazy that if it did you'd call the newspapers.

Which brings us back to Mama. We've just been told that she's as fat as someone who weighs 400 pounds.

How incongruous is the idea of a 400-pound woman in our world? You may not run into one today, but chances are you'll run into a few during your lifetime. Definitely you'll see some on TV. The image is not unlikely.

- *Angle two*: *Unlikely* (Figure 6.8):

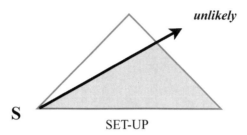

Next we have Mama being as fat as the fattest person in the world. Clearly only one person on the planet can be the fattest person in the world—the odds against being that person are, like, eight billion to one, so, while it is technically possible, I'd say we've moved over to unlikely.

Then we have your mama being as fat as a cow. Here's where we run into a gray area. A huge person may be equal to the size of a small cow. But when we hear "cow" our brains don't necessarily pull up a small cow. After all, the word "fat" is in play, isn't it? Chances are we're going to conjure a full-grown cow.

According to the Internet, Mama would have to reach a good 1,300 pounds to rival the weight of a full-grown cow. It could happen.

But the odds of our running into a 1,300-pound woman (and surviving the crash) are far lower than the odds of running into a woman who is a mere 400 pounds. So much less that I'd qualify this level of incongruity as unlikely.

- *Angle three*: *Impossible* (Figure 6.9):

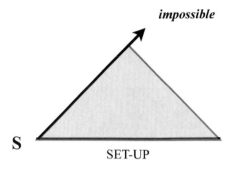

Once Mama grows to the size of a town and beyond, she's clearly reached an impossible size. (Can no one help this woman?)

After "town," we continue to increase the size Mama is being compared to. They are increasingly incongruous, but again, we're stopping this bus at impossible.

Which brings me, of course, to Santa Claus.

Imagine a joke that takes place in Santa's workshop, where he does something cruel to Frosty the Snowman. Now, Santa and Frosty don't exist. It would seem that any joke with them in it would contain an impossible level of incongruity. However, since the joke takes place in Santa's workshop, we work from the rule book that gives us the normative behavior and physics of the North Pole and its fictional denizens. When Santa does something cruel, he is behaving in a way that is unlikely, given what we know about his nature.

We can only know what's impossible if we know the limits of what's possible, based on the physics given to us in the set-up. Sounds pretty obvious, doesn't it?

The set-up isn't always obvious.

Oops.

It's not always easy to identify a set-up, especially in the medium of still image; the nature of the beast requires that both set-up and punchline be presented as a piece. It's up to the receiver to know which is which.

In a famous one-panel cartoon by Charles Addams we are presented with the following information. A skier, making his way up a slope, has turned to see the tracks of another skier. The tracks head directly toward a tree, then split off, each track going around opposite sides of the tree, before rejoining to continue down the hill. When our eyes follow the tracks, we see that they are being made by a man further down the hill, skiing normally.

One may surmise that we are simply being shown a scene that takes place in a world where it is possible for skiers to break the laws of physics. In other words, if it happens all the time in this universe, maybe it's not incongruous.

That's where the other skier, the observer, comes in. He reinforces the notion that the cartoon's reality has been—at least until this event has occurred—our reality. In both our worlds, those tracks shouldn't be there.

WHAT IF . . .?

The real genius in the Addams cartoon is not showing the event. Our minds keep following the tracks and trying to make it work, but each time we short-circuit into paradox. We never find out what happened.

But what if the picture had depicted the skier going through the tree, or if we saw him split in two? Cognitively, of course, this is less interesting, since we no longer have to fill in gaps. We may just look at the whole picture and say, "Okay, here's a guy reacting to a very strange thing. So?"

The event is impossible only because we don't see it. If we saw it, it would no longer be technically impossible. The other skier would be witnessing an event that he had heretofore thought was impossible.

Impossibility within larger narrative contexts

In a larger narrative context, each joke must either conform to the reality of the narrative or it can change the rules.

Something that's impossible cannot happen. Until it does. When a fish starts talking to Bob Hope's character in *Road to Utopia*, it is no longer impossible for a fish to talk. Until this moment, we—and Bob Hope—would have assumed it was. Now we have to assign a new rule to the universe: it contains a talking fish.

This joke, because it causes us to readjust our reality, is the highest level of incongruity: impossible.

But we can only find the talking fish impossible once. What happens if the fish were to talk again later in the film? We would assign the level of incongruity as not unlikely. We already know that this fish can talk.

If a different fish showed up, however, we would have no idea if it could speak. In the film's universe as we understand it, Bob Hope's reaction has told us that he's lived 40 years or so without ever running into a talking fish. Therefore they must be extremely rare, or unlikely.

Note that the rules change for vehicular comedy. If we are presented with a non-vehicular joke in which Mama is the size of Jupiter, the impossibility does not change the rules of reality. The next time we hear a joke in which Mama is the size of a planet, the incongruity is still at an impossible level.

Incongruity outside of behavior and physics

Determining the incongruity level in most situations is not too difficult:

A man walks into a bar carrying a pig. The bartender says, "Where did you get that filthy thing?" The pig says, "I won him at the fair."

Here, the set-up places the action in our world. The punchline shows us an impossible picture: not only can pigs talk, but pigs can win people as prizes. That's high incongruity, impossible.

At the other end of the likelihood spectrum, we may be at a stoplight and see someone in the car next to us singing along with the radio. The event itself has a not unlikely level of incongruity. Our enjoyment may be enhanced by the amount of enthusiasm provided by the singer—there may be violent head and hand motions involved—or the identification we feel with him—perhaps even envy for his abandon. The event causes us to step back and reacquaint ourselves with the inherent incongruity in something we see and do every day.

We may also enjoy added incongruity if the physicality of the singer doesn't match the sound we're hearing—for example, a burly truck driver singing Minnie Riperton's "Loving You."

But how can we use "likelihood of occurrence" to measure a concept like the following:

Knock knock.
Who's there?
Doris.
Doris who?
Doris open. I'm coming in.

Is there likelihood in a knock-knock joke? Do we take it literally? Do we look for incongruity in the fact that someone is telling this joke in the twenty-first century?

What is the picture, or concept, we're left with?

The point is to show that the word "Doris" can double for "door is" when put in the appropriate linguistic frame. There is no other picture being left with the receiver (except someone knocking at a door). The fact is that most words in our language sound like other words, so there's a low level of incongruity there: it's not unlikely that one word sounds like two others.

Does that mean that all wordplay has a low level of incongruity?

I've said it before and I'll say it again: each joke must be looked at individually. All puns, for example, do not automatically get shuffled under any one level of incongruity. The level depends on the incongruity in the finished picture.

Compare the last joke to this one:

Knock knock

Who's there?

Dewey

Dewey who?

Dewey have to keep using these lame knock-knock jokes as examples in this book?

On one level we have the low incongruity of using "Dewey" for "do we," but there's a little more to chew on here. The wordplay is in service of creating a finished picture with a higher level of incongruity. In this case, the joke references itself as an example in a book about comedy—in fact, *this* book about comedy. This is the incongruity of shifting reality, and it notches the joke's incongruity up to the highest level.

Let's take another example, this one the random typo. When a typographical error is in the form of a syntactical mistake or misspelling that does not result in a new word or idea, we don't see a lot of incongruity. People make typos all the time: not unlikely.

But let's say someone makes this simple mistake:

"I needed companionship, so I grabbed some money and went to the god pound."

The incongruity no longer rests on the idea that a typo was made—it's now a typo that has created the god pound, a place where god is kept in a cage, waiting for adoption. Maybe there are even a variety of gods there. The simple typo has netted an impossible level of incongruity.

Kids say the lowest incongruous leveled things—except when they don't

We'll do one more example before moving on. Most of us love kids. Hugely powerful enhancers make everything our kids say and do brilliantly funny—especially their mistakes. Let's estimate the level of incongruity in three kid mistakes:

1 When I was little, I tried to make grilled cheese by putting slices of cheese in the toaster. Nearly burned down the house.

2 One night, years ago, my wife replaced some candles that had burned down to their bases. When her four-year-old son saw them the next day, he exclaimed, "The candles grew back!"

3 When my daughter was two, she wanted to see a glow-in-the-dark toy light up. She pointed to the light switch and asked me to "turn the dark on."

All three of these are amusing mistakes made by kids. Mistakes by kids are not unlikely. The second and third mistakes, however, inadvertently create impossibilities in the minds of the receivers. These aren't just precious misunderstandings—they've created alternate universes that clash delightfully with our own. They both notch up to the level of impossible.

What we can learn about ourselves from an elephant in pajamas

The "shot an elephant in my pajamas" joke shows how systematically our minds work when faced with levels of incongruity. Let's start with the set-up:

I once shot an elephant in my pajamas.

When hearing this line for the first time, we assume that the speaker was wearing pajamas. This seems obvious, but stop for a second: why do we make that assumption?

Because, at first glance, it's the most likely interpretation of the line. However, the line may be interpreted three ways:

1   The hunter is wearing pajamas.

2   The elephant is wearing the hunter's pajamas.

3   The elephant has crawled into the pajamas with the hunter, as a mouse might.

The first version is the likeliest. The second version is on the cusp of unlikely and impossible, and the third is absolutely impossible. All three interpretations are grammatically correct, but we don't even see any alternate meanings until we hear:

How he got in my pajamas, I don't know.

The punchline negates the first meaning:

1   ~~The hunter is wearing pajamas.~~

2   The elephant is wearing the hunter's pajamas.

3   The elephant has crawled into the pajamas with the hunter, as a mouse might.

Most people jump to the next likeliest interpretation of the line and put the elephant in the pajamas. I have met few people who jump to the third meaning. Most of us don't even see it. Still, we can get the receiver there by adding more to the joke:

He probably crawled up the leg while I was sleeping.

Or:

I didn't notice him in there when I put them on

This negates the first two interpretations:

1   ~~The hunter is wearing pajamas.~~

2   ~~The elephant is wearing the hunter's pajamas.~~

3   The elephant has crawled into the pajamas with the hunter, as a mouse might.

Now the receiver is pulled to the final, most incongruous meaning. But notice how we have to be led there. We will always choose the most likely interpretation of information, and when proven wrong we will systematically choose interpretations in order from most to least likely.

This is good to know when you're a comedy writer.

6.3 TYPES OF INCONGRUITY

The three angles may be used to roughly quantify any type of incongruity. The following is a list of a few of the different kinds we may encounter.

[*Note*: There will be overlap in a few of these categories, and in some examples I'm probably splitting hairs.]

Conceptual incongruity

We often hear the phrase "conceptual comedy" used in conjunction with names like Andy Kaufman. In that context, "conceptual" refers to the idea of presenting non-comedic elements to audiences that expect traditional comedy. This forces the audience to be part of the incongruity—it places them inside the triangle.

"Conceptual incongruity," meanwhile, is a much simpler idea. Merriam-Webster cagily defines "conceptual" as "relating to, or consisting of concepts." This forces us to look up "concept," and we find (1): "something conceived in the mind," and (2): "an abstract or generic idea generalized from particular instances."

Long story short, here, if it's conceptual, it's in the realm of idea. If we are forced to construct an incongruity that can exist only in the mind, then it's a conceptual incongruity:

Why was six afraid of seven? Because seven ate nine.

Here we have a conceptual incongruity in that we've given numbers the ability to fear and to eat. As we'll learn when we get to the cognitive process, the incongruity level is not impossible, because the set-up has already created the hybrid of (number + animal characteristic). Beyond this, the likelihood of seven eating nine is difficult to determine. One could argue that the level is unlikely, in that cannibalization among numbers would seem to be a rare behavior—logically speaking, of all the numbers, only "seven" seems to be feared; it uses its unique position before the eight in order to gobble poor nine, so the odds against likelihood must be nearly infinity to one. I can't believe I'm having this conversation.

Attitudinal incongruity

We understand and relate to a certain range of emotional responses to any given stimulus. Incongruous attitudes are those that seem to be outside of the normal range.

Here's an old Woody Allen joke:

What if everything is an illusion and nothing exists? In that case, I definitely overpaid for my carpet.

Here, Woody Allen is the one faced with the idea of our temporal nature, the one grappling with a nihilistic philosophy. Yet, rather than expressing any existential anguish, he unexpectedly used the idea to be pissed off about the price of his carpet. This reversal of the normal order of priorities provides incongruity.

There's an old Sid Caesar sketch in which he's on his deathbed, and as his friends and family mourn his last few moments, the discussion turns to lunch—one of them starts taking the others' orders. Soon the imminent death takes a back seat to people switching their orders around—even the dying man has to suggest they just order a plate of cold cuts. We see the simple priority of lunch become more important than the monumental priority of a man's passing.

We often enjoy watching characters who have inflated ideas of their skills or their popularity. The chasm between who they are and who they think they are can be mined for great comedy.

In dramatic contexts, multiple characters may have opposing attitudes toward a stimulus. While individually the attitudes may not be considered terribly incongruous, the discrepancy between one attitude and the next may seem miles apart, creating a larger incongruity.

In all of these examples, the highest level of incongruity we can get to is unlikely: attitudes are never impossible, only improbable.

Usually in this kind of context, attitude is shown to us through behavior.

Behavioral incongruity

Incongruous behavior is that which is beyond what the receiver considers to be normal or reasonable based on the stimulus.

Behavioral incongruity may be motivated by various factors, such as:

- *Extreme or unexpected attitude*: In 1940, when Bugs Bunny first found himself looking into the barrel of Elmer Fudd's gun, audiences expected him to shriek or flee, or do some kind of big take. Instead, he looked at Elmer, seemingly unconcerned with the gun, took a bite of his carrot, and asked, "What's up, Doc?" Audiences roared. At the time, it was practically inconceivable that a character facing such an obviously life-threatening situation would react so casually. This was definitely unlikely. (Of course, we expect it from Bugs Bunny now because our rule book regarding his behavior has been adjusted.)

- *Physiological causes*: Anyone who's drunk, wasted, sick, exhausted, or hormonal can be a ripe candidate for behavioral incongruity. Once, in a display of hormonally elevated emotions, my wife burst into tears at the end of the film *Space Jam*, when Michael Jordan made the final shot. Don't get me wrong—it's very moving, but come on.

- *Ignorance*: In the movie *Big*, Josh Baskin (Tom Hanks) eats baby corn the same way one would tackle corn on the cob. The scene is enhanced by the actor's performance, our feelings for the character, our identification with his innocent mistake, and our empathy for someone doing something socially embarrassing. Still, it's an easy mistake to make, given the similarity between the two types of corn, so the action has a low level of incongruity: it is not unlikely for a child—and Hanks in this film is a child—to make this mistake.

- *Outside the box problem solving*: Buster Keaton was a master at finding unexpected solutions to common problems. In his short *The Scarecrow*, he's rigged a one room house to function as many different rooms. At dinner, his condiments hang from the ceiling with counterweights, so he and his roommate can easily swing them back and forth for use during the meal. At the meal's conclusion, the entire apparatus is hoisted back up and out of sight. The incongruity for us lies in the fact that this approach to solving the problem is outside our range of experience, and therefore unique.

- *Disregard for social norms*: Our rules of society often discourage us from expressing our true feelings. Irritation with someone who is a pompous blowhard, for example, is something we may all feel but never publicly show. Groucho Marx felt no such obligation to act within social norms. His feelings weren't particularly incongruous, but his decision to act on them often resulted in some great insults and incongruous behavior. As Rufus T. Firefly, the president of Fredonia in *Duck Soup*, he interrupts Margaret Dumont's gushing public welcoming of him to get her to pick a card. When she does, he tells her she can keep it; he's got 51 left. He then showers her with insults about her girth—until he hears she's rich and suddenly shifts gears: "Can't you see what I'm trying to tell you? I love you!" He simply doesn't give a damn about social protocol.

- *Outside motivation*: A character may be forced into incongruous behavior. In the film *Billy Madison*, the title character has to attend grade school again—even though he is an adult—to gain the trust of his father. In *Some Like it Hot*, Jack Lemmon and Tony Curtis have no choice but to dress and act as women to avoid being bumped off by gangsters. In each of these stories, the characters have a goal that can only be achieved through behavior that is outside the norm. *Some Like it Hot* actually does this twice. If Tony Curtis wants to win the love of Marilyn Monroe, he must pretend to be an eccentric millionaire.

When we are shown that the character has no option but to engage in behavior that even he recognizes as unusual, his choices may seem actually logical. Forced into these circumstances, we might do these same things.

Having said that, the fact remains that even our character has to acknowledge that his actions are incongruous. And our enjoyment may be enhanced by our empathy for someone who is trapped outside the norm.

THE BEHAVIOR OF OBJECTS

Objects "act" in ways that create a range of expectation in our minds. These expectations are based on our knowledge and experience of physics.

In *Steamboat Bill, Jr.*, the front of a house falls on Buster Keaton. Keaton is standing at the exact spot where there is a window in the house-front, and so he is left unharmed.

There is a level of incongruity here. Seeing the front of the house, it is obvious that most of the surface area is solid wall. When it starts to fall, we project that Keaton is going to be crushed. The odds of his standing exactly in the right spot are unlikely. The angle of cognitive process is low—nothing for us to solve here. Our reaction may be enhanced by the release of tension built up by our expectation.

Presentational incongruity

You need me to mail you a check. I can mail it in an envelope or I can mail it in a piano case.

Presentational incongruity is like that example. There is a message being conveyed by the source, presented in a way that may be wildly inappropriate to the nature of the message.

Years ago there was a Rice Krispies commercial in which a family has run out of the cereal. The dialogue is mundane—except that it is sung in dramatic opera (an aria from *Pagliacci*).

The Onion, everyone's favorite fake newspaper, relies heavily on presentational incongruity, giving headlines and serious wording to ridiculous stories.

Meanwhile, how do we measure levels of presentational incongruity?

Any message can be delivered in a wide variety of ways without the delivery calling attention to itself or conflicting with the message. There are a thousand different ways to say "I'm happy" without the inflection being incongruous. Likewise, there are a lot of fonts with which one can write "We're sorry for your loss" without the lettering looking inappropriately festive. In order to make this kind of comedy work, the message has to be delivered in a way that you wouldn't ordinarily encounter in nature. Therefore, I'd rank the successful incongruous combination of delivery and message as unlikely.

INCONGRUITY THROUGH INAPPROPRIATENESS AND THROUGH UNEXPECTED APPROPRIATENESS

Imagine we're seeing starving children and the soundtrack is playing a festive "Pop Goes the Weasel." The level is unlikely. (It's hopefully unlikely that anyone would do this.)

This is because we have an understanding of music as language. We know that minor chords can bring us down and that low notes and slow tempos can mean something depressing, angry, or ominous. Because music has a language, it can be juxtaposed against events for comic effect.

Sometimes we can get laughs with soundtracks because they're so unexpectedly appropriate. There's a well-known video of a lemur simply looking into the camera. Suddenly the lemur's eyes—already huge—open wider, and wider, up to being amazingly huge. And they stay that way. This isn't computer-generated, incidentally. The sound underneath the video is the Lucasfilm "THX" sound effect, the tone getting louder and louder and plateauing to match the Lemur's eyes.

The incongruity is still from the joining of unexpected elements, but they work together to create a whole, rather than contradicting each other.

Physical incongruity

This refers to the basic juxtaposition of physical objects—including people—to exploit their differences and similarities for comedic value.

Simply placing a thin Stan Laurel next to a large Oliver Hardy gives us this (not unlikely) physical incongruity.

A giant person with an unexpectedly squeaky voice could be an example of physical incongruity. (While a case can be made for placing this under "presentational incongruity," the voice doesn't have to go against any message—it goes against the image of the person who's talking.)

In Tex Avery's animated short *Lucky Ducky*, two hunters in a boat are pursuing a tiny duckling. At one point the duck picks up the entire boat from the front end and swings it back and forth over his head, bashing it into the water over and over. As if this weren't enough incongruity (impossible), the sound effects themselves are incongruous. Instead of splash, splash, splash, Avery punctuated the violence with a variety of incongruent sounds: Crash! Horn honk! Bell ding! Crash! Gunshot! (also an impossible incongruity.)

Shifting reality

When a character on screen suddenly abandons his narrative world to talk with us, he punctures his reality. This is referred to as "breaking the fourth wall." When it happens, someone within the narrative context is reminding us that we are outside the narrative context.

This may be considered behavioral incongruity, or it may be thought of as the incongruity of shifting reality. The primary difference is that the reality we've shifted to includes us. Regardless, it reaches the level of impossible.

Of course, it doesn't always happen intentionally. Bloopers, as discussed earlier, cause shifts in reality for the receiver.

Likewise, comic strip characters will often break free of their realities long enough to reference other comic strips. Every now and again, a TV character will do a joke that refers to some well-known fact about the very actor playing the part. In a last-season episode of *Frasier*, Frasier is talking with an actress who is tired of playing the same role all the time. She says, "You have no idea what it's like to play the same character for 20 years!" The joke, of course, was that Kelsey Grammer had been playing Frasier for that long. Within the dramatic context of *Frasier*, the line is not a joke at all. It only works when we're yanked out of the narrative context.

Logical incongruity

Now and again, a punchline will cancel out the set-up's logic:

> I'm a pacifist and I'll kill anyone who says I'm not.
> Everyone who's not here, raise your hand.

Logical incongruity takes us into the impossible range.

So bad it's good: intent/reception incongruity

Any attempt at entertainment that misses its mark is setting itself up to be comedy fodder. This is because there is incongruity in the chasm between intent and reception.

We can look at movies that were created with no budgets and no talent, and laugh our heads off at the sincerity or self-importance of the project—it's so bad it's unintentionally good.

But we also have a tendency to do this with entertainment that has worked. How?

Because we change. As a culture we are not kind to earlier versions of ourselves. We rather unfairly hold them up to the same social and cultural rules we have in the present. The disparity creates incongruity. That's how we can laugh at the clothes we wore in the 1970s, or the dancing we did in the 1920s or the educational films we put out in the 1940s, 1950s, and 1960s. (Laugh away, but don't forget to hide your senior pictures from your grandchildren.)

Incongruity of association

When I compare clouds to cotton candy, I'm not stretching the imagination. One can easily see the similarities. Low incongruity. When we begin to draw comparisons that don't have any obvious connections, the incongruity increases.

In Howard Gould's play *Diva*, there is a bizarre comparison between the title character's vagina to Vietnam:

> The woman has her own little Vietnam down there. A lot of good men have gone, and not come back the same.

What happens when an audience hears this line? Some people laugh after "She has her own little Vietnam down there." Perhaps they are already trying to mash the two images together, looking for the connector, and creating incongruous images of their own. Is it vicious and deadly there? Is there some kind of similar terrain? These ideas are at the impossible level of incongruity.

But the punchline actually gives us a satisfying logic to the comparison: the two ideas are related by their effect on men. The odds of finding such a logical connection are low, giving us the incongruity.

The idea of casual sex with this woman affecting people in the same way as a stint in the jungles of Vietnam is unexpected, and hyperbolic. The exaggeration gives us an unlikely degree of incongruity, while perhaps provoking images of hollow-eyed, post-traumatic stress victims who have returned from this woman's bedroom. The laugh may be enhanced by our feelings about the Vietnam War, or the use of it as a reference in a joke—this is not an association one would likely make.

Why unlikely rather than impossible? Because people can actually be traumatized by having sex with the wrong person. We don't tend to think of this traumatization on a massive Vietnam level, but who's to say how deeply one can be scarred by an event? Also, the speaker is not making a literal comparison. He is saying that sex with this woman is like going to Vietnam in that a lot of good men have gone and not come back the same. And that may be true.

7

Cognitive process

7.1 COGNITIVE PROCESS: OVERVIEW

In all comedy reception, cognitive work is required of the receiver. The receiver must have the capacity to understand and assemble concepts. "Bill laughs like a car backfiring" means nothing if the receiver is not aware of the meanings of the words and what their syntactical order implies.

Even the recognition of non-verbal incongruity requires a basic level of cognitive process. We are constantly decoding visual input and comparing the information with the vast storehouse of information in our mental rule books.

Differences in cognitive requirements

As stated earlier, sometimes an incongruous picture is presented simply, with little cognitive assembly required by the receiver. Other times, jokes need to be solved before the receiver can complete and appreciate the finished picture. In those cases, the "getting" of the joke provides a brief cognitive thrill that may add to or even exceed the level of enjoyment we get from the completed picture itself. There is also a level of play recognized when the receiver is required to do some of the assembly.

An increased level of cognitive requirement does not necessarily mean an increase in the funniness of a joke. Nor does any level determine the "smartness" of the joke, whatever that means. There is intelligent humor that can be experienced without the mental effort required by higher levels of the process. Conversely, there are plenty of stupid jokes that require assemblage.

The challenge of estimating levels of cognitive process

Unlike incongruity, which is essentially a continuum from low to high, there is no obvious scale for cognitive process. We can conceive of one; certainly we can see the differences between the most simple and the most complicated jokes, but when we try to build a ladder between the two, we run into trouble. We are left with a lowest and highest rung, with most of our comedy falling through the middle.

So I am going to suggest three broad cognitive demarcations, with a caveat to follow.

To put it metaphorically, a joke is a treasure map that must be followed to find an incongruous picture. Comedy comes in three basic kinds of maps:

1   Straightforward information

     Imagine that this is a map made with arrows. We follow them and
     wind up with incongruity. The arrows may go in a straight line, or
     they may be more complex, leading you here and there and around a
     tree before letting you off at the end. Regardless, we need only follow
     the arrows; it's all laid out for us.

     Example: "I have slow reflexes. I was once run over by a car being
     pushed by two guys" (Woody Allen). Notice that we don't need
     to solve any logic problems to understand the idea that is being
     presented. We merely take in the information and compare it to the
     triggered set-up, in these cases normal behavior.

2   Gap-filling

This map has an arrow missing. Using logic, we construct the arrow and thus the joke.

Example: "Your mama's so fat she has her own ZIP code." In this example, we use logic—a city has a ZIP code, therefore Mama is as large as a city—to create the incongruous image.

3   Recontextualization

This map sends you down a road, then gives you information that either presents you with a dual meaning or sends you backwards down the same road, looking at it differently and thus finding the joke.

Example: "My grandpa wrestled a bear when he was in his nineties. That's pretty old for a bear." The punchline changes the interpretation of the set-up, turning it into the joke.

Within each category there are various levels of difficulty.

And now the caveat:

For the sake of graphic simplicity, these demarcations will follow the pattern we've set up previously (Figure 7.1):

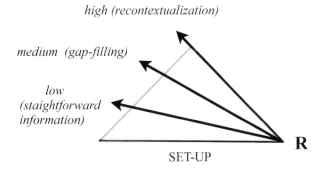

Understand, however, that the categories are broad, and that we are not looking at a straightforward continuum. Some jokes classified as straightforward information may be more complex than some of the simpler jokes that require gap-filling, for example. A more accurate depiction of the triangle is shown in Figure 7.2:

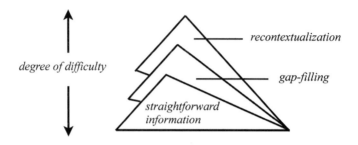

7.2 LEVEL ONE: STRAIGHTFORWARD INFORMATION

Straightforward Information is that which the receiver can understand without having to fill in gaps or alter meanings (Figure 7.3):

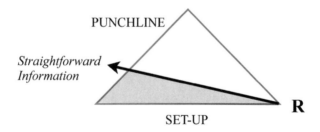

I've already mentioned the house falling on Buster Keaton's character in *Steamboat Bill, Jr.* as having a low level of cognitive process—all the information is on display for the receiver. A simple pie in the face is SI, as is Chaplin's boxing in *City Lights*, Lloyd hanging from the clock in *Safety Last*, or Lucy Ricardo trying to keep up with the candy machine on *I Love Lucy*. This kind of humor is not about our "figuring out" the joke. Having to cognitively unlock a joke can sometimes distance us from the humor. When we do not have to do math, we are free to engage more fully in visceral enhancers, and enjoy a richer vicarious experience.

SI and language

Cognitive requirements increase when we go from showing incongruity to saying things that are incongruous. Language is code, and there are hundreds of formal rules and colloquially understood variations for conveying even the simplest ideas.

We can think of SI humor as that which is made up of concepts and plus signs. Here's that old Woody Allen line again:

I have bad reflexes. I was once run over by a car being pushed by two guys.

Notice that you are not required to solve anything to conjure the incongruous image. Everything is given to you. Here's a line from *Frasier*. Martin has spent an evening with Daphne's brother and heard many stories about Daphne's childhood. Next time he sees her, he asks:

Is it true you wet your pants the first time you saw a Chinese person?

So silly. A straightforward incongruous image. Here's one from a humorous timeline of great scientific achievements:

303 BC: Pelippides devises the theory that history repeats itself. A year later he proves it by devising it again.

When we share anecdotal humor, it is usually at the SI level, laid out piece by piece for the receiver. This next example is a scene from *Seinfeld*, totally SI:

The scene takes place in Jerry's apartment. Kramer, Jerry, and George are present. They are discussing a woman who has been in an accident after being heckled by Jerry in a comedy club:

KRAMER

… she got so upset she ran out of the building, and a street sweeper ran over her foot and severed her pinky toe.

GEORGE

That's unbelievable!

KRAMER

Yeah. After the ambulance left, I found the toe. So I put it in a Cracker Jack box, filled it with ice, and took off for the hospital.

GEORGE

You ran?

KRAMER

No, I jumped on the bus. I told the driver, "I got a toe here, buddy, step on it!"

GEORGE

Holy cow!

KRAMER

Yeah, yeah. Then, all of a sudden, this guy pulls out a gun. Well, I know any delay is gonna cost her her pinky toe, so I got out of the seat and I started walking toward him. He says, "Where do you think you're going, Cracker Jack?" I says, "Well, I got a little prize for you, buddy!" (MIMES BEATING THE GUY UP) Plow! Kee-ya! Knocked him out cold.

GEORGE

How could you do that?

KRAMER

Then everybody is screaming because the driver, he's passed out because of all the commotion. The bus is out of control. So I grab him by the collar, I take him out of the seat, I get behind the wheel. Now I'm driving the bus.

GEORGE:

You're Batman.

KRAMER

Yeah, yeah, I am Batman. Then the mugger, he comes to, and he starts choking me. So I'm fighting him off with one hand and I kept driving the bus with the other. Then I managed to open up the door and I kicked him out of the door, you know, with my foot, at the next stop.

JERRY

You kept making all the stops??

KRAMER

Well, people kept ringing the bell!

Levels within levels

Look at the following examples:

- Scott looks like a monkey.

- Scott looks like a monkey with a hangover.

- Scott looks like a retarded monkey with a hangover.

Putting aside the question of whether or not any of the above is funny (if it's not, maybe you'd have to know Scott, or conjure a funnier breed of monkey), it would seem that each succeeding notion requires more in the way of assembly by the receiver (Figure 7.4):

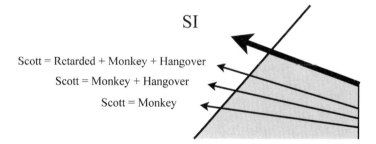

If we were to create cognitive benchmarks for every possible level of assemblage required in comedy, there would be thousands of triangles possible.

But getting back to poor Scott, we can liken him to a monkey in many ways:

- Scott looks like a monkey.

- Scott is a monkey.

With the first line, we are given a statement that may or may not be true. The second line is, on the face of it, false. We know that Scott is not truly a monkey. We hear "monkey" and automatically turn "is" into "has qualities in common with a." This is a commonly understood linguistic short cut. Suffice it to say, *looks like* and *is* are both forms of cognitive "equals signs" and lead to the same basic comparing and contrasting. In other words, both versions are SI.

Source (*pointing to a monkey on TV*): "Look! Scott's on TV!"

Now we are piecing together linguistic and visual references in order to put together the same picture of Scott-as-monkey.

JUMPING IN AND OUT OF CHARACTER

When the source is pretending to mistake Scott for a monkey, he's jumping into a character. It's often more fun to jump into character and act out a joke than it is to simply describe it.

The characters we jump into may be broad or subtle. They may be dumb or evil, or have any trait we impose upon them to help out the comedy. It can simply mean saying a line in baby talk or making a face and saying "this is you." We can take on characteristics of actual people, or affect stereotypes as cognitive shorthand for the receiver. Robin Williams does this all the time. Seriously. All the time.

When a source jumps into character, the change in point of view or the manner in which he or she acts alerts the receiver that the source has gone inside the joke to deliver the comedy from within.

Jumping in and out of character is not a style of comedy; it is merely a technique used to get information across in a colorful way. This technique may be used in the construction of comedy at every cognitive level.

When we point at Scott and call him a monkey, the receiver may have either of these reactions:

1   A conclusion that the source is mistaken or crazy (Scott is not a monkey).

2   Comparison/contrasting of Scott and the idea of a monkey.

When my daughter was little, I could point to a cow and say "Look at that big cat!" and she would laugh. The laugh came from both places: first was my phenomenal stupidity, and second was the idea of the cow being a large cat, perhaps meowing, or trying to lie on a window-sill, or playing with a large ball of yarn in a slow, lumbering way.

Turning up the cognitive pressure in SI

Even with SI, we sometimes have to think about a joke for a few seconds before we appreciate how funny it is. This does not mean we have to decode the line or recontextualize the pieces; it's just that the combinations are unexpected or new to us.

On *King of the Hill*, Dale is describing how wretched the choir is:

This choir is the feces that is produced when shame eats too much stupidity.

There's a lot going on here. First, we have a choir compared to feces ("is" is assumed to mean "is as low as" or "is as repellant as"). Then we get into the actual origin of the feces (apologies to Darwin). The linguistic structure of the sentence forces us to give "shame" the ability to eat—not only eat, but the ability to eat too much. The same sentence forces us into assigning food-like quality to "stupidity." It also tells us that too much of it affects the digestive system (!) of shame, resulting in a specific kind of feces.

—which is then compared to the choir.

Other lines in the same vein:

- This soup tastes like despair.

- 1975 called—they want that haircut back.

Using SI to manipulate connections

Let's go back to that line from George Carlin:

If a cow laughed, would milk come out her nose?

How does the receiver take in this line?

First we encounter the set-up: if a cow laughed. We are being asked to overlay incongruous elements—human behavior on cows—before we even get started on the punchline. We accept this challenge without question. The syntax of if/then demands that we quickly create the provisional reality of a laughing cow.

The brain creates the new combination rapidly, but we don't have time to cross-check every single connection our mind has with "cows" and every connection our mind has with "laugh." We are only creating the hybrid concept to see where the thought is going.

Among the hundreds of connections we have with "laughing," many of us have memories of being—or knowing—kids who laughed while drinking milk, forcing the liquid through the nose. And among the many things we know about "cows," one is that they have milk inside of them. Having already agreed to the existence of the laughing cow, we've given Carlin the keys to both sets of connections, and he's free to link them however he chooses.

When we hear the punchline, would milk come out her nose, our first micro-second thought might be: why would it? And so we take this image (milk coming out of the nose) and run back to the set-up, where we find it connects with both cow and laughed.

By measuring the image in the punchline against the pieces in the set-up, we are, in essence, checking Carlin's math, and we're happy to find that the incongruous image isn't random. There's logic (selective though it is) behind the laughing, milk-shooting cow.

Aside from being able to cognitively enjoy the nod to logic, we're also left with the playful image of a cow laughing, and milk shooting out her nose. (I particularly like the choice of saying "her" instead of "its," encouraging the anthropomorphism.)

This is the basis for all the old "What do you get when you cross a blank with a blank?" jokes. In the set-up you agree to an incongruous hybrid, and the punchline comes from a linkage in the associations you have with the two elements that have been combined (Figure 7.5):

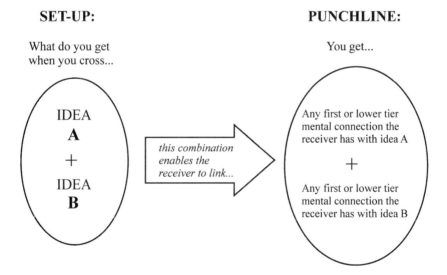

Other examples:

1   We spot someone in a restaurant and, based on his looks, tell our friends, "If Elmer Fudd and Tim Robbins had a baby, it would be that guy." This is A + B = (combination of visual characteristics of A and B).

2   In the movie *Enchanted*, the animated heroine, Giselle, finds herself transformed into flesh and blood and stuck in a very real New York City. Preparing to clean the apartment where she's staying, she sticks her head out the window and sings a little song for all the animals to come and help. This being New York, however, the animals are not cute woodland creatures but the denizens of the city: rats, flies, and pigeons. The premise has mashed an animated being with animation physics into the New York we know. The result is a combination of associations we have with the two. SI.

The if/then (or what-if) structure is perhaps the most commonly used tool in comedy. The full array of concepts can be introduced and explored at this level. When a stand-up comic says, "Imagine if everyone in the world were named Moe ..." and then goes on to tell us all of the delightful complications that would occur in this circumstance, it may be all SI. We can take ideas or dramatic conceits and extrapolate them forever without requiring the receiver to fill gaps or recontextualize.

Building tension, thwarting expectation

Building tension

The building of tension is common to both drama and comedy. We can manipulate the tension of a joke by understanding how and when to reveal information.

If you've ever made a baby laugh repeatedly, you've probably used tension. The first few times you jangle your house keys or make a stuffed animal pop up from behind your back, the baby laughs like crazy. Eventually you sense that the baby is building an expectation, so you start drawing out the time it takes for the funny thing to happen, spending more time on the buildup, or even creating easy misleads.

In the silent film *The Kid Brother*, Harold Lloyd's character—also named Harold—approaches his girlfriend's house. Just as he opens the gate to the front yard, an angry dog comes around the side of the house and dashes for Harold, who is prepared: he produces a cat from behind his back and places it on top of a tall gatepost. Without slowing, the dog changes course, charging and barking at the out-of-reach cat as Harold calmly walks past him to the front door.

It's an ingenious bit of problem solving. But notice when the cat is shown to us: not until the dog is racing toward him at full speed and all appears lost.

They could have done it differently, showing Harold get the idea for the cat and hatch his plan. Or we could have seen him carry the cat in front of him as he walks toward the gate. In these versions you wind up with the same joke, but you'd see it coming. There'd be no tension in the joke, and no satisfying surprise at the last moment.

Surprise! Thwarting expectation

The sequence in *The Kid Brother* is all SI, although one might argue—and this "one" sounds suspiciously like a certain kid in the back—that since the set-up makes you believe one thing and the punchline makes you realize you were wrong, couldn't that be recontextualization? (As you'll recall from the overview, the punchline of a joke that requires recontextualization forces the receiver to go back and see the set-up differently.)

First of all, you're not fooling anyone, kid in the back—we all know it's you. Second, we have to recognize that, by the nature of its definition, any surprise will thwart expectations or assumptions.

Harold Lloyd's placing of the unexpected kitten on the gatepost reveals that he was in control of the situation the whole time, which makes our assumption wrong. We may laugh at being fooled and at Harold's cleverness.

But the laugh does not come from our new understanding of Harold pre-cat. We laugh at what he does with it.

Compare this to another Harold Lloyd sequence, this one from *Safety Last*.

The film starts with a title card, telling us that the fellow we're about to see has witnessed his last sunrise before taking that long, long journey. We then iris in on Harold, looking forlornly at his loved ones through vertical bars. Behind him, a noose hangs ominously. Eventually, the camera moves and reveals that Harold is merely behind a gate at a train station. The noose is one of those old mail-bag holders. He's just going on a trip.

Here, the surprise makes us go back and reorient ourselves. We replace the jail cell and the noose with their new identities, and suddenly everyone's behavior is comedically overwrought in its new context. We would not have seen the humor without going backward and rebuilding.

One might say that a punchline in SI can correct our mental course, but it builds on the set-up and points to a new idea. In recontextualization, the punchline can point backward and make you see the joke that was already there.

Creating expectation in the receiver

There are a few ways for a source to create thwartable (thwartifiable?) expectations. One way is to set up a pattern. It can be linguistic, behavioral, conceptual, rhythmic, even tonal. Once the pattern is established, simply break it.

Jerry Lewis used to get laughs just by speaking off-key. As a society we speak in our own cultural rhythms and singsong patterns, i.e., pitching our voices higher at the end of a question. It isn't strictly singing, but even the most tone-deaf among us can tell when a question is being asked—we all understand the song of our language. Lewis would say something to Dean Martin like, "What song shall we sing first?"—and throw the word "first" off into some flat note that would destroy the expectation of our singsong.

If you've studied comedy even casually, you'll have heard of the "rule of three." This is a common device in which three things are listed or performed, and the third one is funny because it breaks the pattern set up by the first two. Why three, rather than four or five, or a dozen? Because three is the most efficient way to do it. A long list can get tiresome, as well as give the receiver time to see the ending coming.

The rule of three may be found in stories dating back to the dawn of civilization. There are always three brothers or three questions or three pigs, and the third one breaks the pattern. We can find the rule applied in phrases like "hickory dickory doc" or "Wynken, Blynken, and Nod." The linguistic pattern is established and then broken—bang!—by a third, one-syllable punchline.

Here's an example from the film *The Addams Family*:

Morticia cleans out a closet. She finds three bags. The first bag contains Uncle Knick-knack's Winter wardrobe. The second bag contains Uncle Knick-knack's Summer wardrobe. The third bag contains Uncle Knick-knack.

Another way to influence the receiver's expectation is through careful planting of information:

Two Arabs meet on a boat coming to America. Each is excited about starting his new life in the United States. They can't wait to become citizens in this wonderful new land, and as they enthuse, they become competitive—each boasts that he's going to be even more American than the other. Finally, they make a bet. One year after the boat docks, they will meet at the pier and see who has become the most American. The boat docks and they go their separate ways. One year later, they meet up again. The first one says, "I went to Disneyland last week, I went to McDonald's for lunch, and I'm going to a baseball game this afternoon." And the other says, "Fuck you, towel-head."

Everything in this joke has been about the positive aspects of Americana, conveniently leaving out anything ugly. By using language that pulls the receiver away from the dark side of our national identity, the source can knock him over the head with it at the end.

But don't take my word for it. Let's look at the concept of *American* in the mind of the average person (Figure 7.6):

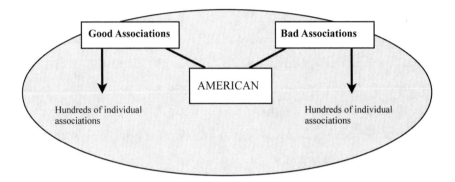

Now let's add all the words in the set-up that might skew the receiver toward the positive side for the mislead (Figure 7.7):

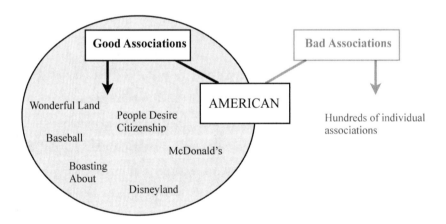

By loading the language toward the positive, the joke pulls the receiver toward the idea that being the "most American" actually means being the "best American". When we're hit with the punchline, we are jerked back into realizing that America has an ugly side too.

Aside from establishing patterns, we can build expectations by borrowing oft-used linguistic or physical patterns, or containers, and breaking them. In Mel Brooks' *The Producers*, Max Bialystock bemoans the fact that his play, intended to flop, has become a hit:

> How could this happen? I was so careful. I picked the wrong play, the wrong director, the wrong cast. Where did I go right?

When we hear the words "Where did I go—" the ear expects to hear "wrong." Circumstances, however, have forced Bialystock to bend to faulty logic and end the sentence differently, thwarting our expectation.

And now we get into basic wordplay.

A word about wordplay and altering containers

The term *wordplay* covers a wide range, although its boundaries are somewhat vague. At what point does clever wording become wordplay? Generally, we recognize it when word juxtaposition calls attention to itself separately from the content of the message being communicated.

In SI, wordplay may enhance a joke, or it may be the point of a joke. Alliteration, for example, may be used in a way that doesn't pull focus from the message but merely enhances it. On the other hand, alliteration can be the joke, as when an incongruous amount piles up in dialogue.

Altering linguistic containers

Our language is packed with well-known phrases. They come in the form of clichés, expressions, song lyrics, quotes, etc. When we encounter certain word orders repeatedly, they become embedded in our minds. Here in America, when we hear someone say "I pledge allegiance—" we have an expectation that the next words will be "—to the flag." When I say, "What you talkin' 'bout—" maybe you will think, "—Willis." There are millions of these. I just picked the two that Americans hold most sacred.

We can think of common word groupings as linguistic containers. They are usually kept intact by the source (to set up an expectation or mislead) except for some unexpected tweak that changes the meaning.

For example, a guy I know once described a group of catty women as:

An embarrassment of bitches.

At first this might look like a pun, but there's no double meaning being employed. Instead, the source takes the linguistic container "an embarrassment of riches" and replaces a single phoneme, which changes the word, which alters the container.

I must admit, I have a weakness for doing this kind of wordplay. It's like doing a card trick. Recently, I was at work when a co-worker looked at her watch and said, "It's only three? I keep thinking it's four-ish." And I said:

"You mean you can't see the four-ish for the threes?"

This means nothing if you don't know the phrase "You can't see the forest for the trees." In fact, it means nothing even if you do—the whole point is using the co-worker's statement to alter a container.

When the daughter of playwright George S. Kaufman told him that a classmate of hers was dropping out of school to get married, he replied:

"She's putting her heart before the course."

He was playing off the old phrase about putting the cart before the horse, switching it around to fit the context of the conversation. The message itself is practically nothing—he merely restates the situation. It's not what he's said that's the joke. It's what he's done.

Containers as triggered set-ups

Notice that the source never says the original phrase that's being tweaked. He only says the altered version. Because of this, he must leave enough of the original container intact to trigger it in the mind of the receiver.

Going back to "embarrassment of bitches" we see that only one sound is substituted in the entire container: an "R" becomes a "B." What if the line were "an embarrassment of wenches?" I suppose it could still trigger the original container, but it's moved further away; it's not as satisfying. If we try "an embarrassment of catty women," we're too far afield to make the line meaningful as a witticism.

Notice, too, that without our knowledge of the original container there is no joke. Imagine if the phrase "putting the cart before the course" didn't exist. Now imagine George Kaufman's daughter saying, "Well, Dad, my friend is dropping out of school to get married," and he replies, "She's putting her heart before the course." I suppose the daughter might just say, "Um, yeah, that's a way of putting it. Nice talking with you. Good luck on those award-winning plays."

This means that the original container is the actual set-up.

Using the Kaufman line as an example, we start with the stated or circumstantial set-up (Figure 7.8):

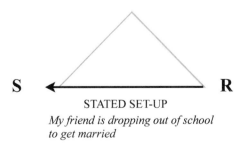

STATED SET-UP
My friend is dropping out of school
to get married

This spoken set-up sends the source off to alter a container (Figure 7.9):

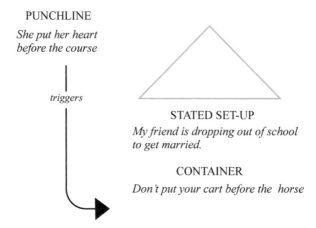

This gives the receiver two set-ups by which to measure the punchline. How incongruous is Kaufman's line to rules inferred from the stated set-up? It's actually not incongruous—he's restating her information.

Now we come to the second set-up. Kaufman's line is measured against the original container. When the receiver does the math (Kaufman did the math, the receiver does it backwards), it can be seen that Kaufman has merely switched two letters (or phonemes), actually keeping every element of the source phrase intact, while managing to give it a meaning that is specific to the circumstance at hand. In the complexity we find our incongruity.

Degree of difficulty and incongruity

Altered containers can be insultingly simple. "In Rob we trust," for example, merely changes the subject of a well-known phrase from God to Rob. It takes us hardly any work to deconstruct it, and so we're not terribly amused or impressed.

Then there's "heart before the course." The change is more intricate, more subtle. We have to get into the individual phonemes to see what's been done.

The more difficult the accomplishment, the greater the odds against it being pulled off. This gives us levels of likelihood, which gives us the spark of incongruity we need to make it a joke.

In the grand scheme of things, it is still a low level of incongruity. We generally look for our primary incongruity in the content rather than the code that delivered it. We are more impressed than amused by linguistic gymnastics unless they are performed in the service of creating a strong, incongruous image or they trigger strong enhancers.

Keep in mind that wordplay does contain the word "play." Our recognition and enjoyment of play is a socially satisfying experience, one that enhances our experience of comedy. Some of you older folks may remember that we discussed a "Laugh-type B" in an early chapter—in this case it might be a laugh of appreciation or applause more than a visceral, content-triggered laugh.

Visual containers

Containers are not limited to language. We can also alter visual containers.

The painting *The Mona Lisa*, to pick an over-parodied example, is a visual container. As a culture, we are familiar with that particular arrangement of shapes and colors. An altered version triggers the original in the mind of the receiver, who will then hone in on the new element and see the painting in a new way.

Compare this to a comical photo of an adult with a large baby's head super-imposed on top of the body. This is a highly incongruous image, but there is no clear container.

A parody uses its target as a container, retaining enough elements from the original to make it the obvious set-up.

* * *

Let's go back to Scott one last time. How about these lines:

- Scott likes to eat bananas while hanging from a branch by his tail.

- "Hey, Scott, where's your organ grinder?"

- Scott's very handsome, from the hair on his face to the thumbs on his feet.

You may think that the above lines give us Scott-as-monkey, but they don't. They give us clues and we supply monkey. At this point, we've crossed into the next angle of cognitive process.

7.3 LEVEL TWO: GAP -FILLING

From here we move to comedy that is presented indirectly. It requires the receiver to fill in a cognitive blank in order to complete the incongruous picture (Figure 7.10):

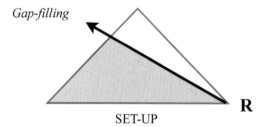

In an episode of *The Colbert Report*, Stephen Colbert looked at the camera and yelled, "Hey liquid paper! Your bottle should say you don't work on computer screens!"

The joke lies not in the content of the line, but in what it implies: Colbert has actually tried to use the stuff on a computer screen and is too dumb to even realize he's been dumb—he blames the product for not warning him.

He never says he did it, we don't see him doing it, yet because we witness his outrage, we contribute the final puzzle piece—the funny part—and enjoy the incongruity. We've filled in the gap.

While a SI joke may present us with both if and then, a joke that requires gap-filling may only provide us with if, forcing us to figure out the then. If Colbert is making this complaint, then it means he has done an incongruously dumb thing.

Gaps based on assumed knowledge

Take this old chestnut:

Your mama's so fat that when she wears white they show movies on her.

The set-up tells us we're looking for Mama's size. When the punchline comes, it contains the words "white" and "show movies on." The brain goes through the connections that arise from these ideas, coming up with the commonality: "movie screen." Having figured that out, the receiver links "movie screen" with the information in the set-up. Mama, it seems, is as fat as a movie screen.

Now that the information is decoded, the receiver can enjoy both the satisfaction of figuring it out and the incongruity of the finished picture. By co-creating the image with the source, the receiver can also experience what we'll call a cognitive thrill.

THE COGNITIVE THRILL

Here's the same information, given two different ways:

1 Your mama's so fat, when she wears white they show movies on her.
2 Your mama's as fat as a movie theater screen.

The first one requires you to fill in the cognitive gap and create the picture yourself. The second one gives you the picture already finished.

▶

> Do you feel the difference in processing the two lines?
>
> Here's how it feels to me. It's like snapping a handful of raw spaghetti in half. In the first example I get to do it myself—snap! In the second, I am merely given two handfuls of half-spaghetti. In both cases I end up with the same thing, but I'd prefer the tactile satisfaction of the tension and the snap—isn't that the fun?

So where, exactly, is the gap? Here it's represented by the box with the question mark. Fill in the gap and you've got yourself an incongruous picture (Figure 7.11):

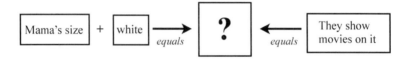

The picture, by the way, is not just of a woman whose size is that of a movie screen. It also contains the incongruous idea of people actually using her for this purpose, which can bring up the enhancers/inhibitors that acompany the scenario. We may enjoy a safe level of sadism and superiority in the woman's humiliation, or we may find humor in the idea that people would go through the extra trouble of using a person to show movies on, rather than find a simpler solution, like using an actual movie screen or a blank wall.

Let's leave Mama alone for a while. The poor woman's been through enough.

In 1933, someone interrupted lunch at the Algonquin hotel to announce that Calvin Coolidge was dead. Without skipping a beat, Dorothy Parker asked, "How can they tell?"

This joke is fundamentally the same as the joke about a woman being as big as a movie screen.

Both are what you might call indirect comparison. The first compares a woman to a theater screen, the second compares Coolidge alive to Coolidge dead. They are indirect because their meaning can only be understood when the receiver fills in the gaps.

Both jokes rely on assumed knowledge. In the first joke, the source assumes you know what a movie screen is and that you can do the math required to piece together the comparison. In the second joke, Mrs. Parker assumes we know that Calvin Coolidge was a notoriously quiet man of low energy, who was famous for going to bed early every night. (Of course, this joke wouldn't exactly kill today, since most people don't know much about Calvin Coolidge.)

Here's a Larry Gelbart line from *M*A*S*H**:

Radar: We're out of toilet paper. It's gotten so bad the men have broken into the fortune cookies.

Can you feel yourself doing the math? I love that he doesn't actual reference the little pieces of paper that the fortunes are printed on. He just says "fortune cookies" and allows us to make the connection.

On the triangle, the joke is as shown in Figure 7.12:

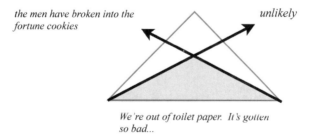

the men have broken into the
fortune cookies

unlikely

We're out of toilet paper. It's gotten
so bad...

The line of cognitive process is at the medium level, and the line of incongruity is at the unlikely level, since the completed image is that of people behaving in an extremely unlikely way.

And, of course, the joke may be enhanced by delivery, gross-out factors, identification with their desperation, superiority, etc.

Filling the gap against your will

As fluid as our language is, we have many parts of conversation that are ritualized. That is, some expressions have automatic responses. If we switch on a TV in time to hear a character say "Gesundheit," we can assume the sneeze that came before. Our knowledge of these rituals can be used to create gaps.

I have a friend who makes some pretty bad jokes. Occasionally, I'll give him an annoyed look after he makes one and he'll pretend as though he's given me a present, saying cockily, "You're welcome." You've probably run into "You're welcome" before. It implies that you've said "thank you" even though you haven't, and usually when it's the last thing in the world you want to say in that moment.

Gaps based on planted knowledge

The set-up may be used to create any rules we wish in the mind of the receiver. Once this is achieved, we can force the receiver to apply those rules in the punchline in order to fill in a gap. To see how this is done, let's start the next joke with the punchline:

> One night the father of a teenaged girl hears a knock at the door. He opens it and a young man says, "Hello, hello, my name is Chuck!" And the man slams the door.

This means virtually nothing. It doesn't exploit any pre-existing mental connections in the receiver's mind. Now look at the set-up:

> One night the father of a teenaged girl hears a knock at the door. He opens it and a young man says, "Hello, hello, my name is Joe! I'm here to take Lisa out to the show!" So he calls Lisa, who comes downstairs and runs off with

Joe. The next week, the father hears a knock at the door and sees another young man, who says, "Hello, hello, my name is Neil! I'm here to take Lisa out for a meal!" So he calls down Lisa, who runs off with Neil.

The set-up gives us the tools to solve the joke. In the world of this joke, it seems, a guy can only take girls out to do things that rhyme with his name. (It's amazing what we'll agree to in a set-up.) Once that pattern has been established, the receiver can use the formula to project what might happen when Chuck shows up.

Notice again that the punchline does not give us the incongruous image. Slamming the door is not the joke. The joke is in the father filling the same gap as we are. And it's only funny because we didn't hear it. If we'd heard Chuck say he was there to fuck the daughter, the joke would just end on an odd note.

In jokes like the Chuck example, most of the fun is that we get tricked into going someplace naughty. Here's another example, this one being a joke that was written—but not used—for the old *Jack Benny Program*: Jack is in a medical clinic, passing the doors of different doctors' offices. He reads each one as he passes: "Doctor Earlich, ear doctor … Doctor Footman, foot doctor … Doctor Ballzer …".

Did any of you notice the rule of three going on there? Anyone besides the kid in the back?

We can establish a pattern in less than three (provided the concept is basic enough) by asking the receiver to complete a simple if/then: "If quizzes are quizzical, what are tests?"

Gap-filling and visual humor

Gap-filling may also be used in still image comedy (I refer you to the long-winded discussion about the Charles Addams cartoon in Chapter 6) as well as comedy that is performed visually.

In moving image, we can leave logic gaps for the audience to fill. Years ago, when Raquel Welch was hosting *Saturday Night Live*, the writers wanted to do a bit where, during her monologue, the camera would keep slowly dropping from her face to her breasts. In this example, the image is not the joke. The image is merely evidence that there's an off-screen cameraman who can't concentrate with Raquel Welch's enormous breasts in the room. The unprofessional and immature behavior is the joke, but the audience must fill in the gap to get it.

We can also create a gap by doing a "cut-to" joke. You've seen it a million times. Gilligan says, "I'm not dressing like a girl. You can't make me. You can't make me, you can't make me—[and we cut to Gilligan dressed like a girl, as he continues]:—you can't make me, you can't make me!" Somewhere during the cut Gilligan either changed his clothes, or they were changed by force. It is left for us to fill the gap.

Exploiting gaps in the receiver's database

Up until now, the gaps we've discussed have been created by the source, either through indirect language or pattern creation. The humor depends on the receiver filling those gaps to complete a picture.

There are times, however, when comedy is based on the receiver not being able to fill a gap. The fun comes from the fact that the gap has been existing all along in the receiver's mental landscape without the receiver's realizing it. I'll explain.

We live in an extremely complex society. On the surface, it may seem to have a basis in logic or intelligence, that there's an order to it somehow. Yet our convoluted social rules alone would send any logic-based alien screaming back into space. Our world is built on a wobbly foundation of religion, instinct, science, and tradition. We don't stand on solid ground; there are logic gaps all over the place. Growing up with them, though, we don't see them. We generally assume there's a logical reason for everything we say and do—until some observational comic asks:

"Why do they put Braille on drive-through bank machines?"

That particular line is from George Carlin. Others have asked:

"Why do they call it Grape Nuts cereal when it has neither grapes nor nuts?"

"Why do cowboys wear spurs on both feet? If one side of the horse goes faster, doesn't the other side?"

"What's another word for 'thesaurus'?"

When faced with these questions, the receiver goes to retrieve the answer from the mental database: after all, there must be a logical explanation for this behavior—some sort of mental connection we can come back with … but it's not there! Or if it is, it's so tenuous we can't find it in the moment.

The receiver has been shown by his own gap that an incongruity exists.

The embedded punchline

In the following diagram, the one-line joke has been broken up into its component parts. As you can see, the words do not fall into the usual order of set-up/punchline. Instead, the punchline is embedded in the spoken line as an instruction for the receiver (Figure 7.13):

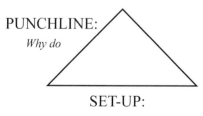

PUNCHLINE:
Why do

SET-UP:
They put Braille on drive-through bank machines?

In effect, *why* is the punchline. It causes us to unravel the logic and reveal the incongruity that was there all along. Because the receiver had to do it, there is a cognitive thrill.

Do not be fooled into thinking that all question-based comedy will break down this way.

WARNING: GRAY AREA

Here again, I must stress that these categories (SI, gap-filling, and recontextualization) are broad. At no time is that more apparent than when we zoom in and look for transitions from one category to another, as though they are connected in a straight line. Somewhere between SI and gap-filling may be a bit of a gray area. Even standard, straightforward language contains many short cuts that force us to make tiny cognitive leaps. How big do these gaps need to be to constitute gap-filling? I can't think of any examples of these "gray area" jokes, but I thought I'd write this so that when a certain kid in the back shows up with a bunch of jokes and starts yelling "What about these?" I can at least say I addressed it somewhere. The kid in the back scares me.

7.4 LEVEL THREE: RECONTEXTUALIZATION

The comedy we've examined thus far has been built on forward motion. The receiver assembles pieces provided by the source and—sometimes doing a little algebra—comes up with the comedic concept (Figure 7.14):

Recontextualization

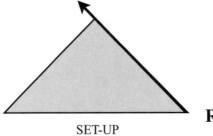

R

SET-UP

Now we get into transformational comedy, in which the punchline contains simultaneous meaning (as in puns or *double entendre*), or humor in which the punchline forces the receiver to go back and look at information from the set-up differently in order to find the incongruous picture. Let's start with the classic:

"Take my wife—please!"

"Please" is the punchline. Its placement is an instruction for us to go back and change the meaning of the words "take my wife." He is no longer offering her as an example, he is offering her to anyone who will take her.

Here's a common recontextualization you may have done yourself (don't lie!) and all you need is:

Some guy trying to read fine print who says, "I can hardly see it."

or

Some guy discussing an inoculation, who says, "I didn't even feel it."

or

Some guy referring to a passing storm, who says, "I thought it was going to be this big dramatic thing and it was over in a few minutes."

And that's where you say:

"That's what *she* said!"

Your punchline has taken the words in the set-up and put them in a new context—one in which their meaning changes to tell a story of the guy being an inept, or ill-equipped lover. The picture may be cartoonishly incongruous, and you have the enhancer of superiority going for you, too.

Gray area: The road from SI to recontextualization

Remember the levels of incongruity? (Yes, yes, kid in the back, we all know you do.) The scale of incongruity represents a simple progression from less to more. Creating demarcations gives us gray areas and room for argument, but the idea is conceptually simple: each level builds on the one before.

Things are a little trickier with cognitive process. If we were to try tracing a progression from SI to gap-filling to recontextualization, we'd hit a wall.

It's easy enough to get from SI to gap-filling. As we leave larger gaps in our communication, more work is created for the receiver. At some gray area we find that the comedy is not fully assembled; we have to do some of the work ourselves because most of the incongruous picture lies in the gap.

But we don't naturally progress from gap-filling to recontextualization—it's SI that actually takes us there (Figure 7.15):

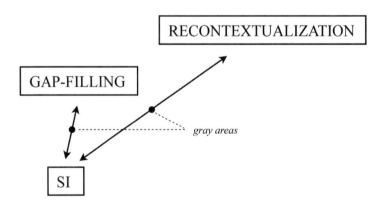

There is a point at which the punchline begins to tamper with our understanding of the information in the set-up. This is the beginning of recontextualization and it starts with the word *not*.

The addition of the negative

Remember the "not" joke? For a while you couldn't go ten feet without hearing it. It's a mean little device. "Sure, I'd love to go to the movies with you—not!"

The last word negates everything that came before it. We'll call this form of joke *negation*.

Compare these statements. Both contain the same information, but in a different order (Figure 7.16):

| The Boss | + | is | + | not | + | happy | (finished thought) |

| The Boss | + | is | + | happy | (we believe thought is finished) | + | NOT |

You can see how the second line will play with the receiver's feelings. Still, notice the plus signs. We are simply adding the negative value in a different place, following our SI instructions and building a mental concept. But the placement is crucial because the receiver has been led to believe the thought has been finished before it's been thrown in the opposite direction.

What helps this work (as much as it can work) is the fact that we speak English—the "not" is intentionally jarring when placed at the end of the sentence. In German sentence structure, "not" is commonly said at the end, throwing the statement into the negative. The Germans' entire language is built on the "not" joke. Doesn't that tell us something about them?

Negation is what you might call the dinosaur ancestor of today's more elegant mislead joke. It's the simplest level at which the punchline is built to make you go back and do something to the preceding information.

More negation: when a joke is not a joke

- What happens to a gray rock when you throw it in the Red Sea? It gets wet.

- Guess who's in the hospital? Sick people!

- How do you get a nun pregnant? Screw her.

The set-up leads you to believe that there is a clever joke answer. The punchline defies expectation and turns it into not-a-joke. The point is to fool you: this is a joke ... not. In the end you are left with the feeling of being fooled, plus whatever enhancers and inhibitors come up from the content, such as subversion or shock in the case of the nun joke. There is also irony in the idea that a joke has been made out of not doing a joke.

Negation in visual comedy

In the movie *Top Secret*, a general sits back in his desk chair while on the phone. His boot-clad feet are up on the desk, crossed in front of him. Finally, he gets off the phone and walks away—but the boots stay in place, crossed and at an angle. They were never on his feet, but have been placed strategically on his desk in such a way as to fool our eyes. The effect is startling and funny—the joke has been played on us. It's like an optical illusion: "this is so/now it's not."

In *Super Hero Movie*, the main character is depressed. He sits in his littered home, a week's-worth of beard on his chin, eating junk food. His uncle finds him in this state and chastises him: "Look at you ... eating junk food ... wearing fake beards ...," and he rips the now-revealed-to-be-fake beard off the guy's face. Again, jarring and funny.

Here's why negation is in the gray area: we don't have to do a lot of math to understand these jokes—in fact, the work is done for us. Leslie Nielson actually tells us it's a fake beard before he rips it off. What could be more straightforward than that? But the punchline throws us backward. It says, "if this is fake, what have we been watching?" The answer reveals the incongruity of someone wearing a fake beard or a general with boots crossed on his desk for no reason. The reveal itself is funny, but the real humor comes from what it implies about the past, which we have to reconstruct by laying new information over old.

SARCASM

Sarcasm is ongoing self-contradiction. When my daughter says, for example, "Yeah, that was real educational, Dad" (words that look good on paper), her attitude clearly conveys the opposite: *Not!* And the delivery wins: I'm an idiot.

This would appear to be negation, but there is an important difference. In negation, the "not" comes at the end of the joke, so it can reverse the meaning of what came before. In sarcasm, words and attitude are conveyed simultaneously. We do not have to go backward.

The incongruity in sarcasm does not come from the self-contradiction, but in the picture created by the sarcastic one. Here's some basic sarcasm used on the SI level:

"Gotta love that 100-degree temperature, huh?"
"Hey, great—meatloaf *again*! Why don't we have it every night until I die?"

Each of these examples paints an incongruous picture (someone loving 100-degree temperatures, someone loving meatloaf to an insane degree) while getting across the point that the source feels the exact opposite, and that the weather, or the meatloaf, or whatever, is stupid.

Of course, sarcasm can be used cleverly. In the film *Arthur*, the title character makes an announcement to his butler, Hobson:

Arthur: Hobson, I'm going to take a bath.
Hobson: I'll alert the media.

Letting the set-up harden as a concept

Look at Figure 7.16 showing the "not" joke. Notice the words between the set-up and punchline: "we believe the thought is finished." In order for recontextualization to work, the receiver needs to be secure in his or her interpretation of the set-up before the punchline forces the receiver to change it. When this does not happen, the joke can land in a gray area.

> My school is tough. Every day I see muscle-bound, tattooed students beating each other with chains—and those are the girls.

Notice the dashes, in which a pause allows the receiver to feel comfortable with his interpretation of the set-up before adding the punchline. There's a great version of this joke in the film *The Four Seasons*. Alan Alda's character, Jack Burroughs, is speaking with his daughter Beth about college:

> Jack: Don't you have any friends?
> Beth: Yes, but all they want to do is get drunk and pee off the balcony.
> Jack: What about the girls?
> Beth: Those *are* the girls.

Jack's line "What about the girls" reinforces the audience's interpretation of the set-up. The set-up, by the way, works really well. "Pee off the balcony" is a great mislead, effectively cementing the receiver's confidence in his or her interpretation of the set-up.

Recontextualization: Going backward

In SI, the punchline may take the receiver in an unexpected and incongruous direction (Figure 7.17):

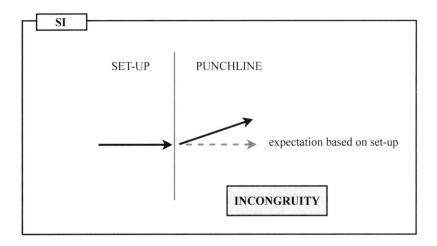

In recontextualization, the punchline makes the receiver look at the set-up differently (Figure 7.18):

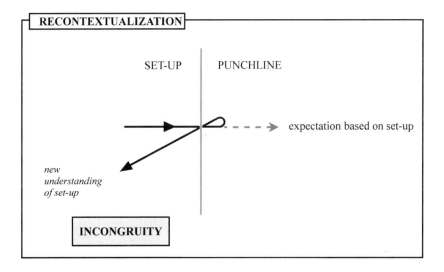

New information changes the meaning of the set-up:

> So this guy from New York has had enough of the big city, and moves out
> to rural Wyoming to make a fresh start. As he unloads boxes into his new

cabin, an old pick-up truck drives up from the direction of his nearest neighbor's house, a mile away. A gruff old man gets out and says, "Howdy. I'm your neighbor. Thought I'd invite you over for a little party this evening at my house."

The man is happy to find the locals so friendly and agrees to come by that night. "I should warn you, " the old timer says, "there may be some drinking." "No problem, " says the city slicker. "I've done my share of drinking before. I think I'll be fine."

The old man says, "Well, there may be some fighting, too."

"Well, I grew up in the Bronx. I think I can hold my own. Thanks for the warning, though."

The old man says, "Oh, and … there may be some sex."

"I think I can be okay with that, "says the man. "So what should I wear?"

The old man says, "Doesn't matter. It's just gonna be you and me."

That joke consists of a set of misleads, pulling the receiver toward the idea of a rowdy, well-populated party. The punchline forces the receiver to see the set-up in a new context—everything that built the image of a party now builds the image of probable rape.

Notice that the joke is not based on a misinterpretation of the set-up. There are no double meanings, either of individual words or of sentence structure. Instead, the punchline gives a new piece of information that we go back and overlay on the set-up with shocking and funny results. And another example, this time from *Cheers*:

Carla: My husband used to take nude pictures of me. Very artsy stuff.
    Until I smashed the camera and broke his nose.
Lilith: You hit him?
Carla: No, I fell off the monkey bars.

A couple more:

- This year, the State of the Union address occurs on Groundhog Day. It is an ironic juxtaposition of events: one involves a meaningless ritual in which we look to a creature of little intelligence to predict the future, while the other involves a groundhog.

- I've been with the same woman for 25 wonderful years. If my wife finds out, she'll kill me.

- A doctor says to his patient, "Mr. Jones, I'm afraid you're going to have to stop masturbating." Mr. Jones says, "Why?" The doctor says, "So I can examine you!"

Words with double meanings

An easy way to construct a recontextualization is to include a word with more than one meaning in the set-up:

On *Frasier*, Niles is—improbably—at a basketball game. He is listening to a transistor radio, and someone asks him what the score is. Niles says, "West Side Story."

As receivers, we take Niles' answer and go back to find an alternate definition of "score." We have to understand both meanings and switch over to the one we weren't expecting.

The first joke of this type that my daughter ever really "got" was when I said to her, "Did you ever wanna fly?" When she nodded, I said, "Okay, then I'll catch one for you." Watching her put it together and start laughing was something I'll never forget.

Notice, of course, that I had to say "wanna," which can be heard as either "want to" or "want a". The punchline changed the meaning from one to the other.

Here's one using the rule of three:

Mama had Hives. Sister had Hives. Papa had Hives arrested.

The addition of the word "arrested" makes us go back and change both "had" and "Hives."

PITFALL ALERT

A quick reminder: simply replacing one word for another does not make it a pun. "An embarrassment of bitches," for example, is merely a cleverly altered container.

In the film *Blues Busters*, Slip Mahoney (Leo Gorcey) asks Sach (Huntz Hall) if his is the singing voice he's been hearing: "Are those golden tones emulating from your kisser?" Of course, he means "emanating." There is no double meaning here. It's just a guy using the wrong word, which is SI.

Alternate interpretations in linguistic structures

As I explained so engagingly back when we were estimating levels of incongruity, the line "I shot an elephant in my pajamas" has three increasingly incongruous, yet grammatically valid interpretations. The punchline forces us to select one of the incongruous alternates as correct. English sentence structure enables us to do this all the time:

She opened the door in her négligé—which is an odd place for a door.

We're often presented with set-ups that are ripe for recontextualization owing to ambiguous wording. In each of these examples of dialogue, notice how the response recontextualizes the language in the set-up:

I like to ride horses and fish. Although it's easier to stay on the horses.

Our language employs many phrases that we don't take as being literal—until we're forced to:

They say that every 15 minutes, a man gets hit by a car. Somebody should pull that guy out of the street.

I have my mother's eyes—in a box under my bed.

Recontextualization and gap-filling

Having established gap-filling as a comedic tool, we can apply it to jokes in recontextualization. Here's a line from the late George Miller:

I once drove the whole way from Ohio to Florida with the parking brake on. Greyhound fired my ass after that one.

Presumably, you can see the recontextualization. During the set-up there is no mention of a bus, and so the brain of the receiver assumes the more likely "car."

But the punchline only gives you clues: Greyhound + firing. We have to deduce that the source was a paid bus driver. Having filled the gap, we can go back and reconstruct the set-up: now the car is switched out for a bus and there are probably passengers suffering through the ordeal as well. Having done the work, we complete the incongruous picture.

One day, two hunters are in the woods, when one of them collapses, unconscious. His buddy can't wake him up. Panicked, he calls 911 and tells the operator, "My friend collapsed while we were hunting and I'm afraid he might be dead. He's not breathing and he won't wake up!" The operator says, "Try to remain calm. Now, the first thing you need to do is make sure he's actually dead." There is a pause on the other end of the line, followed by the sound of a gunshot. "All right," says the man, "now what?"

The gunshot forces us to gap-fill that the man has killed his friend, which only makes sense if we recontextualize the words, "make sure he's actually dead."

See what you did there?

SAME IDEA, DIFFERENT LEVELS OF COGNITIVE PROCESS

Groucho and Chico, in *At the Circus*:

> Chico [producing a cigar]: I thought this cigar was in my other suit.
> Groucho: I wish you were in your other suit, and your other suit was being pressed.

This joke is SI. Each piece is put together in sequence to create the picture of Chico being inside a suit while it's being pressed. Here's the same idea, using recontextualization:

> Frick: My brother's very angry—he just had his suit pressed.
> Frack: What's wrong with that?
> Frick: He was still in it at the time.

Now let's throw some gap-filling in addition to the recontextualization:

> My father ironed all the clothes in the family, but he always hated doing mine, because I'd scream and try to roll off the ironing board.

Notice how each one requires a little more work to achieve the same picture?

Recontextualization and altered containers

About a century ago, I wrote this line for Sam Malone to say to an attractive woman on *Cheers*:

"Is it hot in here, or is it just you?"

The joke uses as its container a well-known phrase "is it hot in here or is it just me?"

In this joke the use of the container is secondary, functioning primarily to create a more thwartable (thwartful?) expectation. In fact, the joke functions whether or not you know the source phrase. The recontextualization is in the double meaning of "hot." This is essentially the same joke as "Wanna fly?" and "What's the score?" (see Figure 7.19):

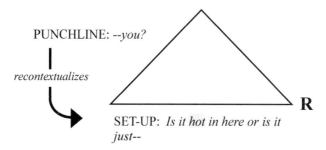

PUNCHLINE: --*you?*

recontextualizes

SET-UP: *Is it hot in here or is it just--*

R

On a *Comedy Central Roast*, Comedian Jeffrey Ross told a joke about the advanced age of actress Cloris Leachman:

She's so old, Shakespeare did *her* in the park.

Once we have our stated set-up, "she's so old," Ross merely swaps two words from the commonly known phrase from every actor's resumé, "she did Shakespeare in the park." By doing this, he forces us to change the meaning of "did," so we have to conjure the image of Cloris Leachman and William Shakespeare having sex in a park. Now we're into recontextualization and high incongruity. The joke gets huge appreciation for being so economic.

Notice, by the way, the italicizing: Shakespeare did *her* in the park. The emphasis tells the audience that there is a twist here—without it, the line runs the risk of being too subtle. It's also more fun to say it with the emphasis.

[*Note*: It's easy to be fooled. The following is a line of mine from *Cheers*, in which Cliff Clavin, the bar know-it-all, defines a Freudian slip:

"It's when you say one thing, but you're thinking about a mother."

By changing one letter of a common word pattern, we've turned a definition of a Freudian slip into an example of one. However, the new word at the end is not an instruction to go back, there are no double meanings. Through straightforward information, we have merely witnessed a character making a very telling mistake.]

Visual misleads

Misleads are not strictly the province of linguistics. We can create the same structure without uttering a word. In *The Idle Class*, Charlie Chaplin, playing a wealthy alcoholic, has just been informed that his wife intends to leave him. Alone in his room, his back to the camera, he shakes as though he were sobbing violently. As he turns to us, however, we see that he is vigorously shaking a cocktail shaker so he can have another drink. We've been set up to believe one thing only to be forced into redefining the action we're witnessing.

Back in junior high school, my class was watching an educational film about the great state of Idaho. At some point, the film cut to footage of an enormous potato—about the size of two pianos—tied to the top of a truck, which was driving through the mud. We all had just enough time to ooh and ahh over the size of this thing when the camera pulled back and we saw what appeared to be an enormous child pulling the truck with—and then we realized we'd been fooled. The potato was merely potato-sized.

In still image, we can expect a receiver to provide the most likely interpretation of a graphic such as the one in Figure 7.20:

Those new to the joke will see a light bulb, while the rest of us know that it's a large woman bending over to put on her underwear.

The *double entendre*

The *double entendre* is basically a joke of the type we've been talking about, but it is up to the receiver to see the second, more racy meaning in the otherwise innocent words. Often, the source cues the receiver, by delivering the line lecherously or with some visual expression that says, "go back and look at that sentence again." We often get them instantly because we humans are a lecherous lot.

Riddles and knock-knock jokes

Okay, I'm going to say it: the knock-knock joke is kind of brilliant. Think about it. It's a fake conversation designed so that the source can make a joke, usually a play on words.

> Knock knock.
> Who's there?
> Delores
> Delores who?
> Delores my shepherd.

Knock-knock jokes started as puns based on names, which makes sense, since a name is the logical answer to "Who's there?" Eventually, the flimsy dramatic pretense dissolved and a whole slew of random set-ups began showing up at the door.

> Knock knock.
> Who's there?

Cantaloupe.

Cantaloupe who?

Cantaloupe without a girl.

These examples require recontextualization, since the receiver has to go back and recontextualize the name as part of another sentence. However, the knock-knock joke isn't restricted to puns. Here's an SI version:

Knock knock.

Who's there?

Interrupting cow.

Interrupting co—

MOO!

Or:

Knock knock.

Who's there?

Control freak. Now you say "control freak who?"

On that note, let's briefly look at riddles.

There are two kinds of riddles: the classic logic problem, where the point is not comedy, but puzzle-solving, and then there's the kind that is built to set up a joke by the source.

This second kind is similar to the knock-knock joke. The source happens to ask how many Polacks it takes to screw in a light bulb. The question is rhetorical—you're not really supposed to figure it out. When you confess that you don't know, the source can tell you that it takes two: one to hold the bulb, and the other to pick him up and turn him around and around (SI). Then again, he may ask how many naked people it takes to screw in a light bulb, finally telling you it's "two, if they're small enough" (recontextualization of the words "screw in").

Interestingly, the "screw in a light bulb" joke went the way of the knock-knock joke; when people got tired of it, they started doing knock-knock-like variations:

Q: How many surrealists does it take to screw in a light bulb?
A: Blue.

Q: How many Jewish mothers does it take to screw in a light bulb?
A: None. "I'll just sit here in the dark."

Somehow, the person asking the question started becoming the person doing the bulb installation:

Q: How many TV development execs does it take to screw in a light bulb?
A: Does it have to be a light bulb?

Homework for the hardcore comedy detective

It would be impractical to attempt the inclusion of every known joke structure in a book. Hopefully, there are enough variations presented here to enable the keen-witted comedy detective to take an informed approach to identifying the cognitive process required by any joke.

When observing comedy, notice where the punchline is in relation to the comedy:

- Does the punchline deliver the funny information (SI)?

- Does the punchline make *you* provide the funny information (gap-filling)?

- Does the punchline make you see that the funny information is in a new interpretation of the set-up (recontextualization)?

8

Variations

8.1 EXPLORING THE FOUR CORNERS OF THE TRIANGLE

Having spent all this effort creating triangles of various shapes, what, exactly, have we created? How does one shape differ from another in regard to a receiver's response?

Interplay between cognitive process and incongruity: Pointing toward a laugh-shape

Let's recap:

The receiver's goal is to find or co-create an idea or image that contains incongruity. This recognition of safe incongruity enables us to enjoy a physiological rush.

This is a primal enjoyment; over centuries, we've sought out ways to give ourselves the chemical rush of relief without having to put ourselves in danger. (Not all of us, of course. There are always thrill-seekers looking for this rush in its purest form.) We crave the drug.

In Chapter 1, we defined this visceral response as laugh type 1. It's the reflexive, bypass-the-brain reaction to the things we find funny. We might also call this the belly laugh or the gut laugh.

At the same time ...

Recognition of higher structures in comedy can lead to appreciation for cleverness, an appreciation for the fun of having been tricked. We often respond to this element of play with what we've called Laugh-type 2. We might call this the head-laugh.

Comedy—even back-to-back jokes in a monologue—can swing wildly between the two extremes of cognitive process-heavy jokes and incongruity-heavy jokes.

The head-laugh and the belly-laugh

The two triangles below illustrate the two extremes of dominance in the cognitive process/incongruity pairing, along with joke examples for each. [*Note*: To illustrate extreme incongruity, we are including both high and medium levels, since medium is the highest level of incongruity we can attain in the real world (Figure 8.1):]

High Cognitive Process /
Low Incongruity

Low Cognitive Process /
High / Medium Incongruity

Examples:

-- *She had nine buttons on her night gown, but she could only fascinate.*

-- *You can lead a horticulture but you can't make her think.*

-- *Kaufman's line about a girl dropping out of school to get married: "She's putting her heart before the course."*

Once all the meanings are worked out, the resulting image is of low incongruity.

Examples:

-- *Steve Martin: "I was born a poor black child."*

--*Tex Avery's Wolf character doing eye-popping, head-shattering takes in "Northwest Hounded Police."*

-- *Laurel and Hardy methodically tearing apart Jimmy Finlayson's house in "Big Business."*

-- *Sideshow Bob steps on a rake for the fourth time in a row.*

-- *As this is being written, there are a number of videos popping up on the Internet that feature people intentionally running into walls. Variations on this are starting to show up – couples holding hands while running into walls, etc.*

-- *Chimps dressed like and acting like people.*

On the left side we have comedy that requires high cognitive process, but nets low incongruity. They are clever jokes, and the humor has to rest on the cleverness of construction. As receivers, we tend to intellectually appreciate these jokes more than we find them funny: head-laugh.

On the right, the comedy takes very little cognitive processing, but the result is high in incongruity. Here the source isn't aiming for the head: he's aiming for the gut. Therefore, we find the gut-laugh, or belly-laugh.

There's a story that Mel Brooks and Larry Gelbart were on a panel discussing comedy. A question came up: What's the difference between comedy and wit? Brooks grabbed his glass of water and splashed it on himself. "That's comedy," he said. The audience looked to Gelbart, who said, "Wit is dryer."

Compare the jokes in triangle form, along with the laugh-shapes they may inspire (Figure 8.2):

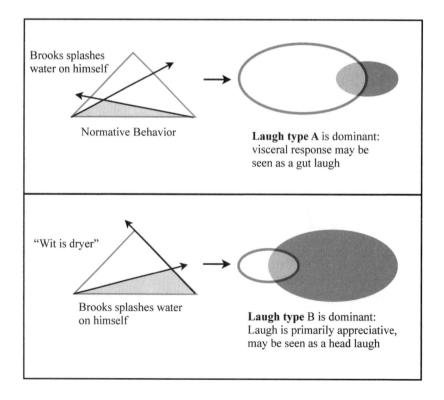

Notice how the first triangle points toward a belly-laugh, while the second swings toward a "head-laugh."

High/high vs. Low/low

Now we compare comedy that has high levels of cognitive process and incongruity with comedy that has low levels of each (Figure 8.3):

High Cognitive Process /
High / Medium Incongruity

Low Cognitive Process /
Low Incongruity

Examples:

-- One morning I shot an elephant in my pajamas. How he got in my pajamas, I don't know.

Emo Philips: "I love to go down to the schoolyard and watch all the little children jump up and down and run around yelling and screaming. They don't know I'm only using blanks."

-- My sixteen year-old sister was named "carrier of the month" by the Times-Gazette _and_ the free clinic.

-- Chaplin seeming to cry, only to be revealed as shaking a drink, in "The Idle Class."

--One day, two hunters are in the woods, when one of them collapses, unconscious. His buddy can't wake him up. Panicked, he calls 911. He tells the operator, "My friend collapsed while we were hunting and I'm afraid he might be dead. He's not breathing and he won't wake up!" The operator says, "Try to remain calm. Now, the first thing you need to do is make sure he's actually dead." There is a pause on the other end of the line,, followed by the sound of a gun shot. "All right," says the man, "now what?"

-- Doctor: "Mr. Jones, I'm afraid you'll have to stop masturbating."
Mr Jones: "Why?"
Doctor: "So I can examine you!"

Examples:

-- We see a baby eat a pickle and laugh at the child's expression.

-- Bill Cosby talks about having dinner with his family.

-- A dog chasing a flashlight beam on the floor.

-- The person in the car next to you singing enthusiastically with the radio.

-- Any scene with Andy and Barney on the porch in "The Andy Griffith Show."

The first thing you may notice when comparing the two columns is that the examples in the right column (low cognitive process, low incongruity) tend to skew toward the softer humor, those moments that most closely reflect real life. This is to be expected—the lower the incongruity, the more recognizable the situation; it becomes less abstract.

So is there a difference in response to comedy at these two extremes?

Indeed there is: comedy with high levels of both variables can get laughs with fewer enhancers than comedy with low levels of both.

As concepts decrease in incongruity, they get to a point where there's not enough conceptual friction to spark a laugh—unless the joke is boosted with strong enhancers.

The high/high comedy is already "out there" as it were, which means it requires less of a boost than comedy at the other end of the spectrum. This isn't to say that enhancers aren't used all the time in high/high comedy. The Emo Philips line above is enhanced (or inhibited) by shock value and violence.

Our appreciation of comedy in the right column is aided by powerful enhancers such as identification, and nostalgia. In Cosby's case there's our feelings for the source, and in *The Andy Griffith Show*, there's our feelings about Andy and Barney. And don't even start me on how we feel about our babies when they make funny faces, or our pets when they struggle with peanut butter. Likewise, we may laugh at the simple notion of a guy with his fly open, and this response may be enhanced if the victim is a pompous jackass who deserves to be taken down a notch.

Here, by the way, we also have the neighborhood of bodily function humor. Simple to think of, low level of incongruity—yet it gets big laughs because of our society's associations to it. Our own hang-ups about our bodies create a tension that is released through joking about it.

Mapping the comedy landscape

Below are the four extreme triangles and how they relate to receiver response (Figure 8.4):

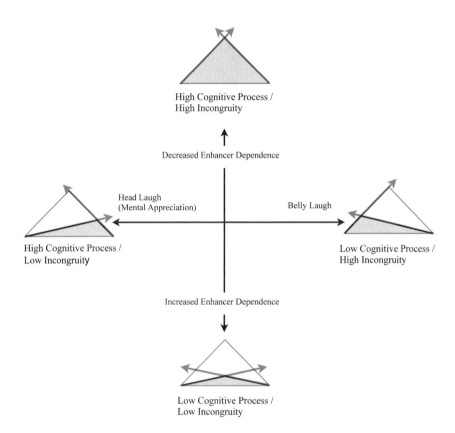

Working from the extremes, we can build a grid using all nine triangles as markers in the comedy landscape (Figure 8.5):

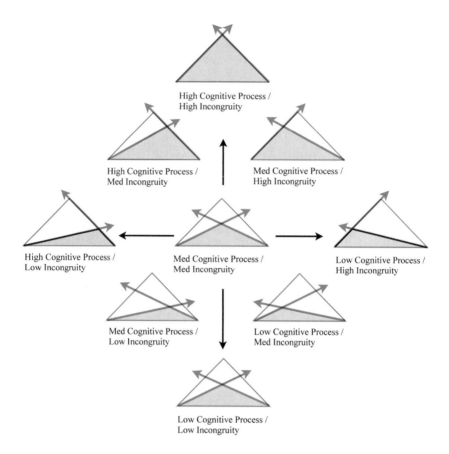

If it seems that we've created a somewhat limited landscape for all humor, consider that betwixt and between these benchmarks are many, many smaller increments of measure. In addition, when we start to add up all the different ways in which comedy is presented and received, as well as the myriad enhancers and inhibitors brought up by each joke, we can begin to see that there are infinite possibilities.

8.2 WHAT ARE PRACTICAL JOKES?

While there are many variations on the practical joke, the most common type involves setting up an unsuspecting target and making him or her believe that fake circumstances are real. This "fake reality" may be installed through simple, spur-of-the-moment acting (faking a heart attack) or they may take months to build and require elaborate props and timing. On the triangle, it goes like this:

- *Step one*:

    A source (the perpetrator of the joke) installs a fake reality in the target's head. This fake reality is at an incongruous angle to actual reality. It may be low ("Now remember, it's a pool party, so be sure to show up in your bathing suit!") or high ("Martians have landed!"), or anywhere in between.

    The receiver is anyone who is in on the joke, including the perpetrator. Using a low level of cognitive process, they measure the incongruity between the fake and the true realities. This completes the first triangle (Figure 8.6):

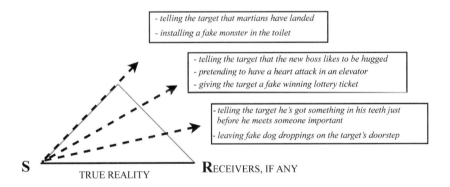

The laugh may be enhanced by the receivers' appreciation for the joke's construction and their anticipation of the target's reaction.

- *Step two*

Once the installation of the new reality in the target's mind is underway, the source moves into the role of receiver. The target unknowingly takes on the role of source.

When the receiver encounters the new reality, he will act in a way that is somewhat appropriate; that is, his reaction will have low incongruity when measured against what he thinks is the truth. However, his response will have a higher level of incongruity when measured against the true reality known by the receivers (Figure 8.7):

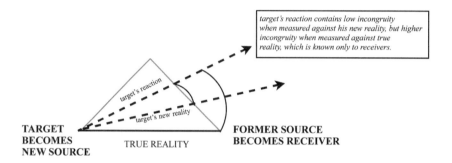

target's reaction contains low incongruity when measured against his new reality, but higher incongruity when measured against true reality, which is known only to receivers.

target's reaction

target's new reality

TARGET BECOMES NEW SOURCE   TRUE REALITY   **FORMER SOURCE BECOMES RECEIVER**

There are often added bonuses to the practical joke. There may be secondary targets—innocent bystanders, who are not in on the joke, reacting to the odd behavior of the target. If you convince someone to show up at a cocktail party in a bathing suit, your target is the guy in swimwear looking like an idiot at the front door of the party. The secondary targets are the people at the party who have no frame of reference for the target's actions. Multiple incongruity.

A variation on this theme is for a source to alter true reality without letting the target know. Place a "kick me" sign on the back of a target, or paint a message on the forehead of your drunken, passed-out friend. He now walks around under the assumption that his reality is unchanged. The world around him, however, adjusts to the new reality, and at some point someone may kick the target or laugh at the victim's face.

Here we have the same basic steps. In the first, a source alters reality, keeping the target unaware. The source then becomes a receiver and the target becomes the source.

9

Comedy and entropy

9.1 SUSTAINING THE LAUGH

Using multiple incongruities to sustain enjoyment

As mentioned in chapter 6, the experience of a joke can lead to multiple incongruities in the mind of the receiver. Seeking out multiple incongruities is a way to sustain that rush of comedic discovery when we encounter a joke. And no one can illustrate this point better than a picture of a man with a baby's head pasted over his own.

Imagine: a figure in a suit stands proudly in some beautiful setting. He would appear to be an adult, but there is a huge baby's head, drooling and blank-eyed, atop the body.

I've watched children look at this sort of mashed-up photo. First they laugh, then they want to see it again, and they laugh again, and as they look at the photo for a longer period of time, the joke starts to run out.

This "joke running out" is a fascinating thing to watch, especially among kids. You see the child studying the thing that was so funny just a few minutes ago, not willing to let go of his or her own expression of merriment, forcing the laugh to keep coming as the eyes dart back and forth from the head to the body, causing progressively smaller bursts of laughter.

What the receiver is doing is trying to keep the comedic rush alive by milking as much incongruity out of the joke as possible. When the dominant incongruity runs out as the fuel for comedy, the receiver starts looking at various secondary incongruities.

The receiver may start by using the body as a set-up and the baby's head as the incongruous element. He or she may then switch sides, using the baby as the dominant idea against which to measure the spindly body beneath (Figure 9.1):

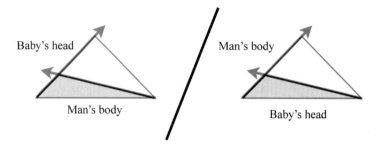

And other possible incongruities (Figure 9.2):

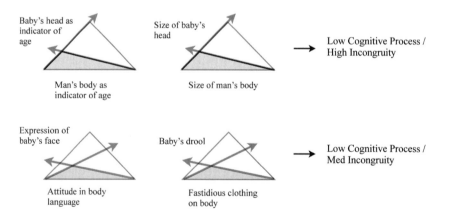

The receiver can also jump out of the triangle and enjoy external incongruities (Figure 9.3):

Knowledge that someone wasted time creating this

?

Understanding that creating mash-ups takes time and energy

→ Low Cognitive Process / Level of incongruity depends on the likelihood of someone spending their time creating this.

Likelihood of that person giving you this picture

?

Knowledge about person who gave you this picture

→ Low Cognitive Process / Level of incongruity depends on the likelihood that the source is the kind of person to present you with this information.

YOUR MAMA'S SO FAT SHE HAS MULTIPLE LAYERS OF INCONGRUITY AND COGNITIVE PROCESS

Let's – for the last time – visit your mama and see how she's doing.

Turns out, she's so fat that when she lies on the beach, Greenpeace keeps trying to drag her back into the ocean.

Let's check out those measurements, so to speak.

First we have to get the joke. By doing some gap-filling, we discover that Mama is the size of a whale: *medium cognitive process, high incongruity*. These are the joke's dominant levels.

Greenpeace keeps trying to drag her back into the ocean

Your mama's so fat that when she lies on the beach...

Now we are free to imagine other incongruities in the picture. For example, we have the notion of grown people *repeatedly* mistaking a human for a whale. There are probably witnesses to this event as well, watching members of Greenpeace trying to drag her toward the water. Since she is human, she is probably trying to fight them off, but the woman is so large, the activists ignore the protests and continue to drag away: *low cognitive process, medium incongruity*.

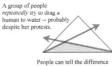
A group of people *repeatedly* try to drag a human to water -- probably despite her protests.

People can tell the difference between humans and whales

Along with that, we have the irony that Greenpeace is an organization whose goal is to protect animal life, yet they are attempting to do something that will probably kill Mama: *low cognitive process, medium incongruity*.

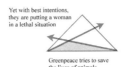
Yet with best intentions, they are putting a woman in a lethal situation

Greenpeace tries to save the lives of animals

Receivers and multiple levels

The fact that the receiver has the option to hold up a joke and turn it around and find various angles of incongruity does not mean he will necessarily do so. Often, we are content to enjoy the dominant level and move along. When collecting data on comedy responses, it is important to note any ancillary incongruities that pop into the minds of the receivers.

Satire and parody: jokes that work on more than one level

A quick clarification:

Parody targets existing art. It can be anything from a sketch that makes fun of a current TV show, or a silly version of Da Vinci's *The Last Supper*. There is no point to parody other than using the source material as a take-off (thus the origin of that phrase) point to create new comedy.

Satire delivers a message wrapped in comedy. It can (but does not have to) rely on a pre-existing piece of art; it can be constructed as original material. It should work as comedy on its own merits, yet enlighten the receiver as to whatever situation the creator wants to illuminate.

Imagine the following scene:

A man waits for a woman in a park. He sees a number of pigeons gathered ominously on a jungle gym. As the man starts walking to his car, a bird flies over him and leaves a large dropping on him. Other birds start flying over the man, who is trying to get to shelter, but they all unload on the poor guy, leaving him spattered as even more birds get in on the sport. Soon, the guy is covered from head to toe in bird droppings.

The scene was from the Mel Brooks film *High Anxiety*. It was done as a parody of the jungle gym scene in Hitchcock's *The Birds*, in which birds are ominously gathering to start killing humans. The original scene is being used as the container for the parody.

This gives the joke two set-ups by which to measure incongruity (Figure 9.4):

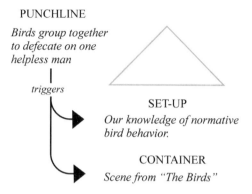

PUNCHLINE

Birds group together to defecate on one helpless man

triggers

SET-UP

Our knowledge of normative bird behavior.

CONTAINER

Scene from "The Birds"

On the first level we enjoy the incongruity of the pigeons' behavior, based on our knowledge of normative behavior for birds. This is unlikely (or improbable to the point of impossible) incongruity, and many people laughed without knowing about the second set-up.

The second set-up is, of course, the triggered container, or the original scene from *The Birds*. Receivers who are familiar with this can compare and contrast the chilling original scene with the silly new one, enjoying the similarities and differences.

Gulliver's Travels by Jonathan Swift is full of comedic plot points, with incongruities that range from not unlikely to quite a few that are impossible.

As we all remember from school, the book is a satire on human nature, government, and religion.

And as most of us don't remember, the book was also a parody of the "traveler's tales" literary sub-genre. If you were reading a lot of books in 1726, you'd have recognized the book as parody.

The story, therefore, can entertain on three distinct levels—yet all cylinders don't need to be firing in order for the jokes to succeed. I read it as a kid purely for the adventure of it. It wasn't until later that I understood it to be satire, which added another layer. And because I wasn't reading a lot of books in the 1700s, I've never appreciated the parody of popular books in that era.

These extra layers act primarily as enhancers to the jokes being told on the surface.

Building the laugh through repetition

Sometimes we seem to run into jokes that get funnier as they repeat over and over. The funniness increases, until suddenly it either becomes boring or irritating. How does this happen?

Here's an example which your not-so-humble author put in an episode of *Cheers*:

> Lilith, a scientist, has to leave the bar. She asks the bartender, Sam, if she can leave a small contraption there until she gets back. She explains that it's a device to detect the IQ of rats. They press one lever and get food, they press the other lever and get a shock. Even the simplest of God's creatures learns pretty quickly how to get the food. She exits.
>
> Now we cut to Norm and Cliff entering from the pool room and coming across this odd device. Curious, one of them presses a lever and gets a peanut. Hey, great. They decide to press the other lever and see if that one gives them a peanut too. But it only gives them an electric jolt. They try it again. Another shock. And again. They can't figure out why it doesn't give them a peanut. "Keep doing it!" And as they keep shocking themselves, their determination increases and we dissolve to another scene.

Once we got the set-up in place, we let the actors, George Wendt and John Ratzenberger, keep shocking themselves for as long as the laughs kept coming. Sure enough, the laughs got bigger and bigger before finally tapering off rapidly.

Why did the same joke get funnier and funnier? Because it wasn't the same joke over and over. It was only the same punchline. Each time the set-up changed. Here's how it went:

The first time Norm and Cliff get a shock, it's not a big laugh—we knew a shock was coming (Figure 9.5):

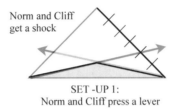

SET -UP 1:
Norm and Cliff press a lever

This first shock now becomes the set-up for the second shock. What are the odds they're going to press the same lever? There's some behavioral incongruity in going back a second time. And yet they do (Figure 9.6):

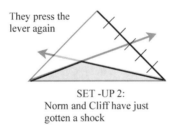

SET -UP 2:
Norm and Cliff have just
gotten a shock

These two shocks are now the set-up for the third: surely they're not going to try it a third time! And they do, so the incongruity is increased again: Zap! (Figure 9.7):

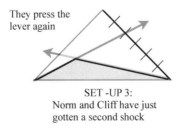

SET -UP 3:
Norm and Cliff have just
gotten a second shock

Three shocks are the set-up for the fourth. Of course, we build in variations—Cliff wants to try now—he wants to try. Watching it, we think, "after three shocks he still—" Zap! Huge incongruity (Figure 9.8):

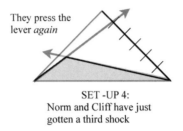

SET -UP 4:
Norm and Cliff have just
gotten a third shock

They show no sign of giving up, and it's all for a peanut—which, by the way, they've forgotten they can get painlessly by pressing the other lever.

Each joke becomes the set-up for the next, the incongruity builds, and the laugh grows.

But, unlike Norm and Cliff, the receiver learns. The set-up eventually changes from "Surely they won't try it again!" to "They never learn." Once this becomes the set-up, the punchline loses incongruity (Figure 9.9):

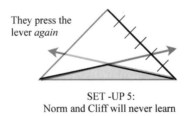

SET -UP 5:
Norm and Cliff will never learn

There isn't a magic number at which this joke starts to wane; it's different for individual receivers. With a large audience, we could feel the laugh losing steam, which told us where to cut out of the scene in editing.

The second wind

I've been in many social circumstances where someone does a joke and it's kind of funny and they do it again and again, and it gets funnier until it dies down. But then, instead of stopping, the source continues to do the bit no matter what. It not only doesn't get laughs, it gets irritating.

And then a funny thing happens: it starts getting laughs again. The joke seems to have a second wind before finally dying again.

This is an illusion. The joke does not get a second wind. The punchline, as always, stays the same, but the incongruity is external. The set-up is now "I can't believe he keeps doing the joke, even though it's not funny." And yet he does, and the incongruity grows again and dies down.

During the first wave, we're laughing at the joke. During the second wave, we're laughing at the fact that the source is continuing to do the joke despite sometimes violent evidence that it has stopped working long ago.

Callbacks

The kid in the back wants to know what a callback is. Anyone who can spot the irony can go home early.

Another way to increase the bang we get from our comedy buck is to do the callback. A punchline or reference is established early in the monologue or the narrative, or the evening's conversation, and then it continues to pop up unexpectedly throughout the piece.

This isn't just repeating the joke over and over. With the callback, the idea is to let the original joke or referent fade in the receiver's mind before a slightly altered set of circumstances yanks it back into focus.

Callbacks can work brilliantly on shows like E Television's *The Soup*, or Comedy Central's *The Daily Show*, in which there's a source addressing the camera while setting up and reacting to video clips. The clips themselves can be called back throughout the show with different set-ups. The sudden juxtaposition of the video punchline grafted onto new verbal set-ups is jarring and very funny.

This is not so different from how we can get laughs out of babies by jangling keys at them. First, we do it a few times, they laugh like crazy; then we pretend to be walking away, building a little tension … only to jangle the keys again! Gotcha!

Takes and reaction shots

A take is a funny reaction. A reaction shot is an isolated shot of a take or reaction.

There are two ways to use reactions in comedy. The first is to create new incongruity, and the second is to reinforce existing incongruity.

Using the take to build new incongruity

A take can serve as a joke unto itself. In *The Jerk*, Navin Johnson, played by Steve Martin, learns that he is a millionaire. His reaction? His head turns 360 degrees. In this example the reaction is the joke.

Takes and reaction shots may also be used in response to information that is already funny, thereby adding a second laugh. One approach is to do a reaction that is extreme enough to provide another layer of incongruity to the situation. You may recall the old comic strip tradition of punchlines being told to characters who react with beads of sweat flying from their heads. (Sometimes, characters would be so affected by the punchline that they'd fly backward out of the panel, with only their feet sticking up into view.)

Throughout history we've seen spit takes, double takes, triple takes, delayed takes, straight men slapping comics, and slow burns. I'm sure there are more, and, if you want to learn about them, enroll in that film history course down the hall.

Using the reaction to reinforce existing incongruity

Let's say a joke has just been executed. Rather than allowing someone to do an extreme take, adding new incongruity, what if we show someone reacting to the joke in a more realistic way, in effect tracing back and reinforcing the original incongruity?

This type of reaction shot has been a staple for years. On stage, it was learned early on that a straight man could double laughs by reacting to the insanity of his partner.

On *The Golden Girls*, the producers found that they could get an extra laugh by going to Bea Arthur for reaction shots. First, they might have Rose (Betty White) tell some pointless story or make an observation using faulty logic. Big laugh. Then they'd cut to Dorothy (Bea Arthur) simply staring at her. The audience would roar. The distance from normal to silly had been retraced, leaving the audience back where they'd started. The round trip doubled the laugh.

The shot is like an echo—the joke takes us from normal to crazy, and the reaction takes us from crazy back to normal.

The differences in reactions are shown in Figure 9.10:

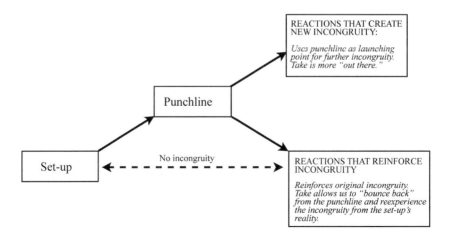

Making the round trip and then some

We can have it both ways, if we wish. When Stan Laurel does something particularly dumb, and Oliver Hardy, exasperated, looks into the camera, his attitude is entirely appropriate—but he's breaking the fourth wall to show it to us, forcing a shift in our reality.

9.2 ENTROPY

Face it. Jokes get old. Comedy structures become hackneyed. And there's nothing we can do about it. In this section, we'll take a brief look at comedic entropy for individual receivers as well as for our culture as a whole.

The inevitability of entropy

Often I talk about comedic entropy with people—why am I not invited to more parties?—and I've gotten some interesting questions:

1 But bodily functions are always funny, right?

   This is a misleading question, in that it isn't about any individual joke. Rather, it's about an entire topic—specifically, our bodies and how we control and don't control them within polite society. As with any topic, every kind of joke can be constructed around it. Oh, trust me, as long as there are enhancers such as shock and love of gross-out humor and identification and superiority and subversion of society, and as long as the junior high schooler in every man tries to be funny, there will be humor about bodily functions. The individual jokes themselves may grow old, but people will find new roads of humor here long before they figure out how to kick our nation's dependence on oil.

2 How come I can laugh at a scene in a movie over and over, even though I know what's coming?

The answer is buried in the question: you're watching a scene. This is where the wonder of the dramatic context comes in. In order to suspend disbelief, the receivers must buy into the reality of the film— even if they know the film by heart. In the dramatic context of the film, the characters do not always expect the comedy that's coming. Therefore, vicariously, it's new to the receiver, who can paradoxically enjoy the anticipation of the joke while being "surprised" by it through his participation in the narrative. In this way, we can still laugh at the jokes we know are coming.

Notice that we don't seem to enjoy the telling of a linguistic joke over and over. Without the suspension of disbelief, we don't have a strong pull to vicariously experience the punchline. Once we've heard it, the stand-alone joke's days are numbered.

3 Does that mean people can watch a scene an infinite number of times without the comedy getting old?

I can't speak for every individual, but I can share something I've seen many times, and even experienced myself. It's a theory of entropy in narrative comedy and it goes like this:

Sooner or later, we all watch Larry

In the previous section, we discussed how receivers might seek out extra levels of incongruity in jokes to keep the laugh going. The same thing happens when people watch movies repeatedly. Sure, we can all enjoy the same funny scene over and over, but eventually the familiarity begins to outweigh our ability to vicariously re-experience the comedy. So we start exploring other incongruities to keep our romance with the scene alive.

We may start evaluating the actor's performance. After that we may start looking for other elements in the scene to piggyback onto our enjoyment of the jokes we know too well.

Watch a movie with someone who's seen it a million times. They'll get to a scene they love and say things like, "Watch his face when he does X," or "Look at that one extra at the back." Generally it means that this person has loved this particular scene many times and has started poking around for fresh incongruities.

I first noticed this phenomenon when I was a kid. Back then, TV channels used to run Three Stooges shorts relentlessly. I was never really a fan, but I knew people that had seen them dozens, perhaps hundreds, of times. Once they knew the scenes by heart they'd start watching the background actors, or they'd look for mistakes in the film. By the time they got around to watching Larry, they were scraping the bottom of the incongruity barrel to keep the scenes fresh. So that's my theory: sooner or later, we all watch Larry.

AHA!

About six months after I wrote the above, I saw voice actor Billy West being interviewed about the Three Stooges. He's a huge Larry fan and described the exact same phenomenon of working his way down the ladder before he began watching Larry in all the scenes.

Personal changes in sense of humor

Clearly we do a certain amount of evolving when it comes to humor; otherwise the big comedy hit of the year would be *The Jangling Keys*, a movie in which someone jangles keys at the camera so we could all laugh like babies do. In fact, there wouldn't even need to be another comedy produced. *The Jangling Keys* would win the Oscar every year.

Unfortunately, for any studio that has *The Jangling Keys* in development, people do move on.

I went through a rebellious phase as a teenager. Not rebellious against the rules of society, but against the rules of comedy. I've seen other teenagers go through it as well, along with some adults who get stuck there. The manifestations were as follows:

1   I decided I found stupid jokes hilarious to tell. By "stupid," I mean things like, "Why did the boy throw the clock out the window? He wanted to see time fly!" At the time, I found ironic humor in the idea that anyone would find this funny. I remember telling jokes like this and even being condescending when people didn't "get" how funny it was that I'd be telling jokes like this. It was a derisive, teenage version of a road that would be taken more thoughtfully and successfully by Steve Martin, who we'll get to shortly.

2   I decided that incongruity was funny just for the sake of incongruity—I didn't even need ideas to connect anymore. The more incomprehensible the ideas were together, the more "funny" it was. If someone asked, "Why were you late today?" I might respond, "Because African elephants can weigh up to 330 pounds at birth."

At that age I was destroying rules without rhyme or reason, and creating no rules to take their places. I hereby thank everyone I know for not beating me senseless every day I went through that phase.

Entropy and incongruity

How many times can we jam two disparate ideas together in our minds before the incongruity of the pairing wears off? Does it wear off?

Take "I once shot an elephant in my pajamas." How many times do we have to hear that before the idea of an elephant in someone's pajamas is no longer incongruous?

Answer: it's always incongruous. And it's always incongruous at the impossible level.

So why does it stop being funny?

Keep in mind: A joke's angle of incongruity represents the likelihood of occurrence, based on rules indicated in the set-up.

An elephant wearing pajamas or Mama being as big as a small town will always have the same amount of incongruity when measured against the norms of real life. Being overly familiar with the joke cannot change that, even if it does detract from the laugh (Figure 9.11):

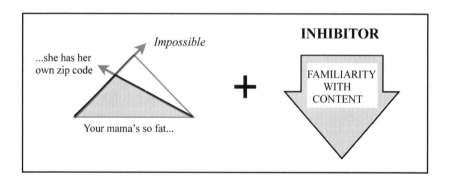

I said earlier that we do not "resolve" the incongruity; we celebrate and maintain the cognitive distance between concepts. Our making the connection does not bring them closer together, but repetition can reduce our delight.

We're speaking now of self-contained jokes, like "Two guys walk into a bar," "I shot an elephant in my pajamas," and "My wife's cooking is so bad." Because it is understood that these jokes are self-contained, we do not carry over rules from one joke to another. Rodney Dangerfield could tell an hour's worth of jokes about his wife's cooking, and after each one our rule book for the set-up would reset to normative behavior. There is no ongoing dramatic throughline forcing us to alter our rule books.

Don't believe me? Having just told a joke in which Mama is an impossible size, let's do another:

> Your mama's so fat that when she goes to the amusement park, families agree to meet in front of her if they get separated.

Through gap-filling, we see that Mama is pretty much the biggest thing at an amusement park, including, presumably, all the rides and attractions there. This is the dominant incongruity, made no less incongruous by many previous jokes in this book bout her size. Our rules reset.

When ongoing comedy forces rule changes

When the joke is part of a larger dramatic context, repetition of a joke forces the receiver to alter the rule book. We touched on this briefly in 2.3: incongruity regarding Mr. Ed and a talking fish in *Road to Utopia*. We also showed how the rule book changed when Norm and Cliff refused to learn on *Cheers*.

In 1941, when Bugs Bunny first looked into the barrel of Elmer Fudd's gun and casually said, "What's up, Doc?" the audience found his behavior very unexpected—and very unlikely. Over the years, through repeat viewing, we've made a rule change: Bugs Bunny says, "What's up, Doc?" when faced with danger.

Even though it looks the same now as it did in 1941, it is actually a different joke, because the inferred rules of the set-up have changed (Figure 9.12):

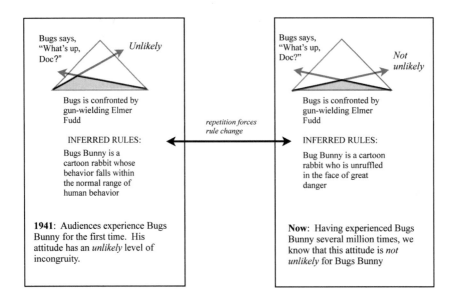

A person coming to this joke fresh would have the same inferred rules as a theatergoer in 1941.

Notice how specific and logical our adjustments are. We always choose the smallest possible shift: when faced with Norm's and Cliff's behavior, we do not adjust our belief to "people don't learn." We make it about Norm and Cliff, rather than changing our view of the normal human learning curve. Likewise, watching Bugs Bunny over and over didn't teach us "it is normal for people to be casual in the face of death." We adjust our definition of Bugs rather than change our global view.

Incongruity is dependent on the norm

Incongruity exists only when measured against a norm. In real life, the norm is an evolving set of definitions. As such, levels of incongruity fluctuate over time. In my lifetime, I've seen the idea of a home computer go from impossible to unlikely to not unlikely. On the other hand, the idea of hearing a record needle skipping has gone from not unlikely to unlikely.

Entropy and cognitive process

Back when we were still slogging through the section on recontextualization, I used many examples of jokes based on double meanings and misinterpretation. Whenever I hear one being told, I often sense the slight pull for me to believe a set of circumstances so that I can be turned around by the punchline. I can feel the deliberate omission of the word one would normally use in favor of a word that is less specific, and therefore open to misinterpretation. Not only can I spot those moments, but once I do, some quick math will point me to some approximation of the punchline. This does not happen 100% of the time, of course; I can still be surprised. Still, I have a pretty good average. At this point it would be sad if I didn't.

So what is going on in my head? After literally thousands of jokes, I'm seeing the structure of the joke underneath the content.

I believe this is a factor in the recent decline in popularity of the multi-camera sitcom. American viewers, for the better part of a century now, have been bombarded with millions of jokes from movies, radio, stage, television, comics, etc. Just the sheer number of sitcom episodes seen by the average viewer growing up in the 1970s, 1980s, and 1990s is easily in the thousands—and each episode contains maybe around a hundred jokes.

Chances are that you've been exposed to thousands of misleads. There are variations, of course: they can be set up by the source, set up by a third party, they can be visual, verbal, hybrid … they can be about any topic, and can have different levels of import in the narrative context.

Even so, after years and years and years of flogging these joke structures, viewers are starting to sense a sameness beneath. They may not be able to put their fingers on exactly why it feels that way, but I think the structures are finally starting to show.

Repetition makes the work rote

Jokes based on gap-filling and recontextualization rely on problem solving, which provides a cognitive thrill, boosting the enjoyment of the joke. What happens when the receiver no longer needs to do the math?

When I say "two plus two equals ...," you will probably think "four" without actually going through the mental process of adding a quantity of two to another quantity of two and counting it all up. This is similar to when we read. As children, we are taught to sound out words letter by letter, but eventually we come to recognize words on the page without having to work our way through them— until we come to a new word, at which point we revert to sounding out again.

So it is with both gap-filling and recontextualization. How many of us still go through the steps of solving "I shot an elephant in my pajamas?" Once we've solved the equation, we've solved it. Mama has her own zip code. We get it!

Gap-filling and recontextualization are the real victims of entropy. When easy math and familiarity take the work out of solving the joke, it can be frustratingly easy to complete.

When collecting data on comedy response, it is important to know how familiar the joke is to the receiver. Has he or she skipped to the ending, forgoing the cognitive thrill? Has familiarity caused him or her to approach the joke with a different set of inferred rules than other receivers?

"That's funny"

When jokes are pitched in a writers' room, they may be met with laughs, silence, or even derision. But often they're met with a nod, or a cursory "that's good," or "that's funny" and it goes into the script. I've seen non-professionals do this as well.

This acknowledgment is sincere, yet it's not a laugh. It's a recognition that all the markers are in place to make the joke work. The receiver may not be moved to laughter, having experienced similar jokes too many times before, but he or she still sees the joke as working. This may be the edge of entropy.

Pushing the triangle to new places

When jokes start to feel too standardized, someone usually pops up and shows us how to push the triangle to new places, extending its possibilities while surprising the public. Sometimes these new places are dead-ends, and sometimes they can lead to massive changes in comedy.

Backtracking: setting the stage for change

In the late 1950s and the 1960s, American comedy started getting its teeth back. World War II had united the country in such a strait-jacket of patriotism that no jesters were able to unleash comedy-coated anger at the powers that be. McCarthyism sealed the deal: if you criticized the American way of life in anything but a congenial, but-seriously-isn't-the-president-doing-a-great-job kind of way, you were a communist. Not that the public at large were interested in having their country criticized—419,000 sons and husbands had just died to preserve it.

But comedy, like music, can't be quiet for long. While Elvis Presley was throwing the nation into a panic with his sexually charged performances, Lenny Bruce was making a name for himself as a counterculture comic. He shocked and challenged audiences by doing comedy about politics, drugs, even abortion. It's difficult now to appreciate how shocking this was.

I won't get into a whole history of comedy here. Suffice it to say that we soon had Mort Sahl and Dick Gregory and other comedians shaking America awake with politically and socially oriented comedy. Woody Allen talked about existentialism and his neuroses. White Americans began discovering the underground records of Redd Foxx, recorded in the 1950s, while *Mad Magazine* introduced sick humor to their kids. During this boom, comedy was reinfused with the almost forgotten blood of social conscience: satire and shock.

Of course, this revolution was content-based. No one was using the triangle differently: it was just the delivery system for more challenging material. The point was to juice up receivers' enhancers and inhibitors.

While this was going on, some comedians challenged comedic structures, steering away from traditional comedy and into performance art. Comedians like Albert Brooks were doing bits that made fun of traditional comedy. Comedy was becoming its own conscience, turning on itself for becoming too slick, too mainstream, too cheesy.

Steve Martin: resurrecting dead triangles

Steve Martin saw entropy as an opportunity. Stepping back, he found that there was something funny in being the last person to believe there was life in a dead joke.

So Martin became a comedy grave robber. Balloon animals, bunny ears, fake arrows through the head … these things are funny to kids, and even then, not for very long. The cognitive processes were SI, and the incongruity had long ago ceased to be entertaining. They were, in effect, dead triangles, no longer viable as props for professional comedy. Yet Martin produced these on stage as though they were unquestionably hilarious. In fact, he referred to it grandly as "professional comedy!"

And it worked big. Of course, the audience weren't laughing at the balloons or the ears or the arrow. They were laughing at the man who was so unstoppably clueless as to present these relics as comedy.

This is not to imply that this was the only trick in Martin's comedy bag. It is one, however, that helped define him nationally.

It is noteworthy that Martin was canny enough to see the entropy even in this approach. Once audiences had caught onto his character—the guy so clueless he didn't know the difference between living and dead jokes—he could explore the persona, use it as a source for any type of comedic idea he chose to explore.

It's also worth noting that his third starring film, *Dead Men Don't Wear Plaid*, was assembled from clips of old black-and-white films stitched together with new footage to create an original plot. The device allowed Martin to interact with performers who were, in many cases, long gone—he got new life out of dead performances. And having done that he moved on.

Andy Kaufman: putting the receiver in the triangle

Around the same time that Steve Martin was stepping back and putting ironic quotes around old comedy, Andy Kaufman was exploring a daring and audience-unfriendly approach.

He forced his audiences to be part of the joke. Rather than just being passive receivers, they were now unwitting participants in the comedy.

How did they become participants? By daring to expect traditional comedy. Kaufman used this expectation as his set-up. He then created incongruity by not giving them traditional comedy. A famous example: once he had gained fame as a character on the sitcom *Taxi*, audiences flocked to his shows, hoping to see him behave like his TV alter-ego. When he didn't, people began to shout out requests—even outright boo him. As "punishment" he read to them from *The Great Gatsby*, starting at page 1. After a very long time, he offered the audience a choice: he could continue reading, or he could play a record. When the audience chose the record, Kaufman put on a recording of himself reading *The Great Gatsby* from exactly the point where he'd left off.

Who's really the receiver in this joke? It seems that the audience were too upset to appreciate their roles in the creation of comedy. It's almost as though

234 WHAT ARE YOU LAUGHING AT?

the true receiver is anyone who hears about this event after the fact. Kaufman and his audience formed two legs of a triangle that can only be connected by someone outside the joke; it's conceptually funny that someone would treat an audience this way—it's the ultimate thwarting of expectations—but being inside the incongruous picture isn't always fun. What we have, in essence, is a practical joke.

Like Steve Martin, Kaufman had more than one tool in his comedy kit. His drive to experiment with the conceptual bounds of comedy took him in and around the triangle—sometimes too far away from it for the tastes of most people.

The future of entropy

Comedy grows old a lot faster than it used to.

There are two reasons for this. The first is the endless flow of information into our heads from every medium. Once a joke form becomes popular, we're saturated with it at a level unthinkable to people a generation ago.

The second is parody. Sometimes the parody is a homage, but in the past few decades empathy has been drained from parody. It's become more derisive. It's just so darned easy to make fun of things!

In today's world of instant comedy, something original can only exist for a split second before there's a parody of it on YouTube or *Saturday Night Live*.

What has this done to the way in which we perceive comedy?

It's teaching us to look for formulas. Parody often compares successful shows or films to other shows or films, exposing structural similarities ("They're just ripping off *Family Guy*"). Parody is also quick to jump on anything new and run it into the ground.

Case in point: remember that shot from *The Matrix* where everything freezes and the camera spins around? It was cool for about a minute, and then the parodies came.

And once something's been made fun of, it's just not that cool any more. Parody destroys its target, turning new ideas into hackneyed ones. This instant hacknification is shortening the length of time we enjoy comedy before we make fun of it or pull the curtain back to expose the structure beneath.

Even now, as any successful film comes out, there's some producer or writer from the Scary Movie/Epic Movie/Date Movie school ready to put the most memorable, innovative moment into his or her piece of garbage parody.

The point is: the more this is done, the more we find ourselves noticing formulas instead of enjoying the rides which comedy has to offer us. Comedy has become its own target.

Portable comedy and straightforward information

The advent of easy-access video is changing the national average of cognitive process levels in portable comedy. For centuries, portable humor (e.g. humor you could carry with you and exchange with your friends at will) was limited almost exclusively to the linguistic joke. For generations, guys have walked into bars, people have responded "who's there" to "knock knock", and everything imaginable has screwed in a light bulb. This portable comedy averaged highly in the top two levels of cognitive process: gap-filling and recontextualization.

Now, there's a huge shift going on. I didn't realize it until my wife pointed out that people just aren't telling that many jokes anymore. Instead, they're sending links to short videos. These videos are becoming the new portable humor, and, because they don't rely on linguistics, SI comedy is becoming increasingly prevalent in the national average.

PART THREE

ENHANCERS, INHIBITORS, AND ASPECTS OF AWARENESS

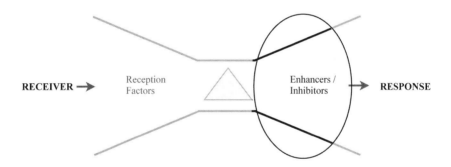

Now that the incongruous idea has been assembled by the receiver, we look at the possible enhancers and inhibitors that may be triggered by the joke's content, structure, context, and transmission.

10

How comedic information triggers enhancers and inhibitors

10.1 OVERVIEW

Enhancers as dominant response factors

Once we intellectually understand the idea created by the triangle, any number of emotions may be triggered. Some are so powerful that they become dominant factors in the laugh, far surpassing the impact of the raw information in the triangle itself. Over the years, this has fooled people into thinking that the enhancer is the joke, or that certain common enhancers are the basis for all comedy. (Yes, philosopher Thomas Hobbes, I'm talking about you. All comedy is not superiority, and just knowing that makes me feel superior to you. Now how funny is superiority?)

Let's look at a Bill Cosby monologue. His material is generally SI, and his levels of incongruity are low. He may spend a hysterically funny half-hour re-creating a saturday afternoon with his brother. Here are just some of the reception factors and enhancers that come up when a receiver takes in a joke that Cosby performs live (Figure 10.1):

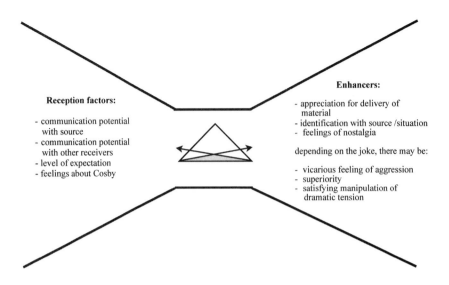

Reception factors:

- communication potential
  with source
- communication potential
  with other receivers
- level of expectation
- feelings about Cosby

Enhancers:

- appreciation for delivery of
  material
- identification with source /situation
- feelings of nostalgia

depending on the joke, there may be:

- vicarious feeling of aggression
- superiority
- satisfying manipulation of
  dramatic tension

The good comedy detective knows that the manipulation of emotion is arguably the most powerful tool in the comedy arsenal. By and large, people respect intellect, but they connect with emotions (brain = respect, heart = connect). For years, writers on *Frasier* would break their necks crafting intricately structured jokes, dialogue, and situations. And people admired the writing. But what did they love? When the dog would stare at Frasier. They also loved Niles being in love with Daphne.

Are they enhancers or are they inhibitors?

Although some factors will trigger predictable effects—physical noise, for example, is an inhibitor—generally, the enhancing or inhibiting is in the eye of the receiver. For example, one may find subversive humor distasteful, while another finds the same humor tapping into his or her own sensibilities or pent-up frustration with authority.

Limits on listing enhancers/inhibitors

Left unchecked, a researcher may attempt to determine the effect of every individual letter of a written joke, the thickness of every line in a still image, each phoneme of a spoken witticism. Likewise, one may try to chart the receiver's state of mind for each second of a five-second joke.

Then we have the brain's facility for making connections. Each mental connection made during a joke leads to another tier of connections, which leads to another. How far down do we go before the feelings evoked by these connections have no impact on the response to the joke? And how specific are we to get with "feelings" anyway?

Well, rest easy, kids. We'll explore the elements that tend to influence receivers most and let the professionals carve those up into even smaller elements in their own time, after we all go home.

Those pesky emotions

I will make a delineation, if only to justify my terminology: "Emotions" will be used to refer to basic individual emotions: anger, shame, joy, etc.

I will also use the broader "feelings" or "feelings of" to refer to standard individual emotions (anger, shame, joy, etc.) as well as commonly recognized combinations of emotions, such as superiority. The recognition of superiority (and consequently, inferiority) brings up an array of emotions such as anger, shame, anxiety, disdain, envy, pride, and joy. This array constitutes "feelings of superiority." "Feelings of moral outrage" would also be shorthand for a combination of emotions.

10.2 ON-GOING SOCIAL NEEDS: SUPERIORITY, IDENTIFICATION, AND INCLUSION

Superiority

Superiority as an ongoing social need

As stated earlier, superiority is not a specific emotion. It is a social state we cognitively recognize, and that recognition triggers emotions.

Unlike most emotions, which seemingly swim around in our psyches waiting to be triggered by outside stimuli, our hunt for superiority is a constant, active thing, motivated by inside forces rather than triggered by outer ones.

As humans, we relentlessly compare ourselves with each other in a world where there is no exact equality. In the pairing of any two people we find variations in attractiveness, intelligence, confidence, tastes, skills, and talent. We note similarities, we note differences. Where there is inequality one may find superiority. In any conversation we can detect subtle shifts in the upper hand. Perhaps every human interaction is actually a battle, or at least a contest.

The fact is that superiority isn't a necessary ingredient in comedy—it's an existing ingredient in all social interaction. It's just who we are: we have the antennae up. When comedy, drama, or social circumstance manipulates that ongoing need, the response can be electrified.

Superiority and comedy

Superiority pops up so often in comedic themes and receiver response that one could assume superiority is comedy, or at least a necessary ingredient.

This notion would certainly be supported by the fact that so much humor involves a target—someone who is made to look foolish by the joke. In comedy, the definition of "target" has vague borders. Sometimes it refers to someone mentioned in the joke. Other times it includes anyone who sets up a punchline, or even anyone in earshot who happens to be misled by the set-up and surprised by the ending.

Comedy can be enhanced by the instability of superiority. The teller of the joke manipulates the information, so he or she is in control—and then he or she tells a self-deprecating joke, and the receiver feels the rush of sudden elevation to superiority over the person who has control. In a comedic vehicle we root for the underdog to gain superiority against an adversary, and when he does it with a joke, our response may be elevated.

Superiority as an enhancer

To find comedy that relies heavily on superiority, we need look no further than YouTube. Recently, I found a number of clips from the game show *Who Wants to be a Millionaire?* that would seemingly support the "comedy as superiority" argument. They were titled "Worst 'Millionaire' Contestant Ever"! and "First Question Wrong on 'Who Wants to be a Millionaire' and 'Who Wants to be a Millionaire' Stupid Woman". These are clips of people missing the first—and easiest—questions on the popular game show.

The viewer comments are largely along the lines of "that person is retarded" or "ha ha ha ha" as receivers gleefully heap scorn upon the hapless target.

Obviously, there's superiority in play. Sometimes we project a certain smugness onto the people who've been selected for these shows. Inside, we may feel inferior to the contestant and resent him for that. When he fails, we get the rush of superiority and he gets the punishment he deserves for having thought himself special in the first place.

By adding our own ridicule in the comments section, we can anonymously indulge the darker side of ourselves and practice a bit of safe sadism, joining the dominant group to cast out the unworthy. Kill Piggy!

While superiority is the dominant enhancer in the popularity of these clips, it should be pointed out that people make mistakes on game shows every day. There are tens of thousands of wrong answers in the annals of TV. Why isn't every one of these posted on the Internet for a clamoring, bloodthirsty audience?

Clearly, failure is not enough. Spectacular failure is more fun. We feel more superior to a person who misses an easy question than to someone who misses a tough question.

But consider: the easier the missed question, the higher the level of incongruity in the situation. It's nearly impossible to miss the easy question. When someone does, we recognize the incongruity—he missed *that* one? (mental recognition) and revel in the superiority—what a moron! (triggered feelings about the event).

The Three Stooges made a living whacking the hell out of each other. Put aside your own opinion of whether or not they were funny—they must have made some people laugh, because they went on whacking the hell out of each other for decades. The audience response was probably enhanced by feelings of aggression and superiority.

Compare that to an audience watching a boxing scene from *Rocky*. All the enhancers of superiority and aggression are there—the crowd get terrifically excited. But the context of a boxing match has made the violence congruent. There isn't laughter.

Repackaging tragedy as comedy

A couple times in my early twenties, I made jokes to my friends about starving children. I am not proud of this. Maybe I was seeing how far I could go to shock people or how dark I could get. The primary enhancer for anyone who laughed was total shock at the incongruity of someone making fun of such innocent and helpless victims. There were other enhancers, such as the delight of subversion, relief at the idea of cutting something so tragic down to size as fodder for a joke, and even superiority, in the form of my friends' moral superiority over me. Sometimes people laughed because it made them feel brave to do so, as if it were a show of toughness. They laughed at the squeamishness of other receivers, feeling superior to them.

Did they laugh out of superiority to the starving children? It's hard to say. These same people, myself included, would probably be reduced to tears if we encountered even one of the thousands of starving infants and children in the world. We turned them into a concept and then laughed at the idea of someone making fun of the concept. The reality is too horrible—the actual superiority too unpalatable—to be seen as comedy. Footage of starvation-wracked villages does not get laughs without some kind of repackaging. (*Example*: If your roommate pretends to howl with laughter at footage of a starving family, the joke is his heartlessness rather than the footage itself.)

There is an old expression: "Tragedy plus time equals comedy." This simply means that a certain amount of distancing has to occur before the public will laugh at a tragic event. But distance is not enough. No matter how long ago it happened, a tragic event doesn't get a laugh by itself. It has to be packaged comedically in some way, like being used as an incongruous counterpoint.

Identification

I'm watching a guy on television having the same argument with his wife that I've had a million times with mine. I can relate to the guy.

Identification is the recognition of one's own personal traits and experiences in other people or circumstances.

By identifying with the man on TV, I assume some inside knowledge of his mental and emotional state, having gone through the same actions myself.

This enhances my involvement with the scene; I now have a personal stake in its outcome.

It also makes me feel less alone, since I'm seeing others in the same plight I've been in.

Have you ever seen a stand-up talk about his relationship, and then seen the audience members laughing and nodding and pointing at each other? They're all identifying. By acknowledging this among themselves, they become unified with the source and each other. It's a pleasant experience and one that enhances the joke.

We can even identify with characters who do things we'd never do, as long as we understand their emotional drive. When Frasier tells a lie that spins out of control, he may behave in ways that are foreign to us, yet his fear of getting caught, his aversion to shame, his need to protect the feelings of others, are all relatable. As long as the episode keeps reminding us of those emotional touchstones (and plot complications prevent him from acting normally), we'll relate to a man doing insane things.

There is a down side to identification, of course. We not only identify with characters who have our good qualities, but also with those who have our less attractive traits as well. Humor that gets too close to our self-loathing, insecure core can be more uncomfortable than funny.

We can even identify with more than one character, or with conflicting sides of a situation.

Identification as an amplifier of emotions

Unlike superiority, which triggers a somewhat recognizable array of feelings, identification can trigger or amplify any emotions. It depends on the element with which the receiver identifies, and on the receiver's history with that element.

(*Example*: My identification with Ralph Kramden from *The Honeymooners* will amplify my enjoyment of the show. Meanwhile, my wife's identification with Alice Kramden will amplify negative feelings for the show. The stronger the identification, the higher the amplification.)

Because we constantly project ourselves onto others, seeking similarities as well as differences, identification, like superiority, may be considered an ongoing social need.

Inclusion/Exclusion

Another ongoing social need involves our desire to be part of the group. Our awareness of inclusion or exclusion is another trigger for emotions. If we get the inside joke, or sense that we are among the hipper part of the audience, we'll have feelings surround our inclusion, as well as feelings about those who are excluded. And if, God forbid, we're the part of the audience who doesn't get the joke or feels left out, we'll have a set of feelings about that too. No one wants to be out of the tribe.

These go beyond feelings of superiority to include the seeking of approval with the source or other receivers and the fear of being a target or outcast.

10.3 ASPECTS OF AWARENESS

It is not enough to say that a joke causes one to experience feelings of superiority. After all, to whom does one feel superior? A character in the joke? The teller of the joke? An audience member who was the target of the joke? Other receivers who didn't get the joke? These are all very different from each other.

When we come into contact with comedy, we don't simply laugh at the content. We respond to the joke in relation to several *aspects of awareness*. These are the ways in which we see a joke and its impact simultaneously. This multi-level point of view multiplies our possible enhancers and inhibitors. Three people may laugh at the exact same joke, but the dominant factor in each of their responses could come from entirely different aspects of awareness. Same joke, same response, different universes.

For example, I'm watching *Saturday Night Live* with my wife's family. There's a sketch in which someone insults the President of the United States. Simultaneously, I have:

1   Awareness of the joke's reality: I experience the content of the joke.

2   Awareness of the impact of the joke on its vehicle: the joke may have an effect on other characters in the sketch, or it may build or release tension in the scene.

3   Awareness of the nature of the joke from my reality: this is my critical recognition that I am receiving a joke. I may measure it against other jokes.

4   Awareness of the joke as it relates to/affects my reality: I may be aware that my mother-in-law is offended by the language in the joke.

5   Awareness of the joke's effect on others as measuring device: I could feel superior to my father-in-law, who took a while to get the joke.

With each aspect comes increased opportunity for triggered feelings and associations.

The aspects of awareness are shown here:

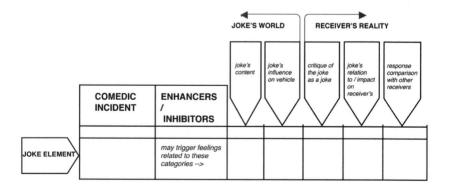

The joke's world

The first two aspects of awareness have to do with the internal world of the joke and its vehicle. The joke's reality may mirror our own or be an entirely foreign construct.

The receiver's reality

The four aspects on the right take place in the world of the receiver, the world in which we recognize the joke as being a joke. From this point of view we can critique it, as well as register its impact on the world around us.

From these two basic points of view we find our aspects of awareness. Feelings relating to these aspects may be self-directed (shame, embarrassment, fear, joy) and/or outer-directed (anger toward, admiration for, envy of). Note that the existence of an aspect of awareness does not necessarily mean that a receiver will have any enhancers or inhibitors in connection with it. There may be a mountain of feelings and associations brought up in one aspect and nothing in another.

Working our way from left to right, we have the following.

Aspect of awareness 1: The joke's content

If Bob is telling me the joke about a guy walking into a bar, then the joke's world contains a guy, a bar, and whatever happens when the guy walks in. At this aspect of awareness, I respond to the content of the joke only. The joke's world does not include Bob or me or my reality.

Imagine that, instead of a joke about a guy in a bar, Bob either tells a funny story that involves himself, or Bob does something funny. I will now respond to Bob in two ways: as a character in the joke's content (first aspect of awareness) and as a teller/performer of a joke in my reality.

(*Example*: I'm finishing up lunch with Bob at a restaurant, when I notice unfinished food on his plate, and say, "You wanna box for that?" Bob says, "No, I think you'd win. Just take it.")

The joke's content contains both Bob and myself, but when Bob pretends to misunderstand me, he is creating a new reality: one in which he would actually think I meant "box" as "fight." From the first aspect of awareness I accept that reality, and enjoy the subsequent incongruous image of the two of us slugging it out for half a sandwich. From my own reality I will critique the joke and admire Bob's quickness.

The joke's world does not have to be entirely separate from our own reality. When an observational comic points out silly things we do, or when someone relates a hilarious story about something that happened at work, then elements of our reality have been packaged as a joke.

Triggered emotions

Some jokes are constructed out of emotionally neutral material ("You can't see the fourish for the threes"). Others contain emotionally charged elements. We may have feelings for them as a society (two black guys, the pope, the president …) or have a personal connection with something in the content (Dad walks into a door). Heightened feelings about a joke element will enhance or inhibit response.

(*Example*: A joke is told that makes the president look like an idiot. It's very possible that the laugh will be much stronger for those who hate the president, and much weaker for those who love him. Yet they are hearing the same joke—and if you switched the material so that the target was his opponent in the last election, you may find some reversal in response.)

One never knows which element of a joke will trigger a strong emotion. Years ago I was out with a small group of people, some of whom I didn't know very well, and I made some offhand joke, which I can't (or won't—I'm not sure) remember after all this time. But I do recall that it had the word "decapitate" in it. And why do I remember that detail? Because as I found out, one of the people there had a mother who'd been murdered a few years earlier—by decapitation. The rest of the evening has been mercifully deleted from my memory. You really don't come back from that.

Aspect of awareness 2: The joke's influence on the immediate vehicle (vehicular comedy only)

This aspect of awareness concerns the joke's dramatic context. This is not the same as the receiver's reality: in a play, the joke's context is the dramatic world of the play, while the receiver's reality is the experience of sitting in a theater watching a play.

Within a larger creative construct, an individual joke can serve a number of dramatic purposes. It can be used to amplify tension or release tension. It may reveal information or attitudes that make us feel differently about characters in the piece. Any of these functions will affect how we respond to the joke.

In the *Frasier* episode "To Tell The Truth," Niles learns that his estranged wife made their family fortune from the manufacture of urinal cakes. Niles says, "Tell Maris I've flushed out her family secret."

The line works beautifully, but not just because it's a clever line. Throughout many episodes leading up to this one, Maris has been bullying Niles through their lawyers, bleeding him dry and threatening to ruin him. When Niles realizes that this family secret gives him the upper hand, his joke is a declaration of triumph. Dramatically, the audience have been waiting for this moment. The satisfying shift in superiority and the release of tension is like rocket fuel to the joke, and you can hear the studio audience cheer through the laugh.

The way we respond to the joke's influence on its immediate vehicle is similar to how we respond to the joke's impact on our reality. We may enjoy the impact of Groucho's insulting Margaret Dumont in the same way we enjoy the impact of Bob's insulting a waitress. It's just that the world of the vehicle is always removed from our own; there's always a wall between the vehicle's reality and our own, which may give us the distance we need to enjoy our more subversive feelings.

The joke's influence on the vehicle includes its influence on any audience packaged within the vehicle, say, a studio audience. As we've established, the laughs we hear on a sitcom are part of the packaged entertainment, and are therefore part of the vehicle.

In 2006, Stephen Colbert spoke at the White House Correspondents' Dinner. In his monologue, he made some delightfully subversive jokes about George W. Bush, who sat a mere few feet away.

Members of the audience who were present that night experienced an in-person performance. Bush being in the room was part of their reality—a reality of which they were extremely aware.

I, meanwhile, watched the whole thing on video. The president and the members of the audience were not in my reality, but part of the packaged vehicle. For me, the impact of Colbert's jokes was indeed amped up by Bush's presence: the joke's influence on the immediate vehicle.

Why am I being so dogmatic? Two reasons:

1   To stress that the vehicle's reality is not my reality. The jokes' effect on Bush had nothing to do with my actual reality, which consisted of me and a computer monitor.

2   Because the level of anxiety, glee, discomfort, etc. that a receiver will feel at a joke's impact on others will be in relation to where he or she stands among them. If I were in the room during that monologue, the tension (for me) would have been high—I don't know if I'd have had the nerve to laugh. Watching it from the safety of home, however, takes Bush out of my reality, and puts him in the vehicle, so I can laugh evilly throughout, even though I still feel a little bit of anxiety.

We may still compare ourselves to vehicular audiences—one might feel superior to them or be annoyed by their level of enthusiasm—but they should technically be considered part of the vehicle, just as a receiver might feel superiority over a character in the narrative.

Aspect of awareness 3: Critique of the joke as a joke

Back to Bob's "guy walks into a bar" joke.

Now I look at the joke from my own true reality; there is no guy, there is no bar. Instead, there's a joke that Bob is communicating to me. I have feelings and opinions about the effectiveness of this joke—as well as Bob's performance—based on previous experiences with comedy.

When a receiver takes in comedy that he's heard a million times before, his recognition (and subsequent feelings of irritation, frustration, or anticipation) comes from this aspect of reality, in which the joke is being compared to other jokes.

In addition, when a receiver notices structural elements of the joke, he is operating from his own reality. The joke's reality (content) has no awareness of how it is structured; one can only look at such things critically, from outside the joke's reality.

Elements of a joke can trigger feelings from more than one aspect of awareness. For example, let's look at some of the feelings that might get kicked up when the punchline of a scene is "I sure don't want any fucking french toast!"

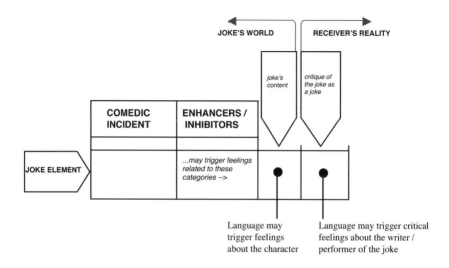

This is also the aspect of awareness from which we appreciate the joke's delivery. And, of course, the delivery of a joke can sometimes be part of the content, such as when Droopy Dog looks at the camera and groans, "I'm happy." When this happens, we respond to delivery both as part of the content and part of our critical assessment of the joke as a joke.

Is the joke "in character"?

The receiver always notes the level of congruity between the source and the comedy. When a joke is "out of character" it may affect the laugh. A nun making a filthy joke may be extra funny because of the exterior incongruity of the joke coming from her mouth. In vehicular comedy we may see a smart character make a dumb joke or a kind character make an insensitive one and the incongruity may be jarring, inhibiting the laugh for an otherwise funny joke.

Another example: After stumbling through the woods at night, friendless and hungry, the hunted monster in *Young Frankenstein* bursts into the home of an old blind man, who is desperate for companionship. What should be a sweet tableau goes awry as the old man inadvertently spills hot soup on the monster, shatters his wine mug, and even sets him on fire.

From a receiver's first aspect of awareness, he may feel sympathy and frustration on the part of the monster, as well as pity for the old man.

From his own reality, he may critique the performances by Boyle and Hackman. He may admire Boyle and Hackman, as well as Mel Brooks (the director) and Brooks and Gene Wilder (the writers).

Aspect of awareness 4: Joke's relation to/impact on receiver's reality

As the receiver of Bob's joke, I will be aware of the joke's level of appropriateness to my reality. Are we at a party? A funeral? The level of appropriateness can have a huge impact. How many of us have ever found something hysterically funny simply because we weren't supposed to be laughing?

I will also be aware of changes in my reality after impact. Did the joke change the tenor of the communication? Did it lighten the mood? Break the ice? Create or add to tension between us? Did he make the joke while I was trying to be serious?

When there are multiple receivers, their very existence may color our reaction to the joke. We may hear material that we would ordinarily laugh at but now it offends us on behalf of others—we may think it's inappropriate for some of the receivers, or we may feel embarrassed because Grandma is present.

Imagine that a source makes a joke at the expense of a receiver other than yourself. You may feel sorry for the victim, perhaps even feeling uncomfortable on his or her behalf. On the other hand, you may join in the torture through loud laughter, gleefully enjoying your superiority and aggressive behavior because it's masked in the pretext of comedy. You may even feel both sets of emotions at the same time, one set enhancing while the other inhibits.

And when you're the target, you will be very aware of other receivers. You may be humiliated and shamed, but you may also feel the excitement of being the center of attention.

All of these possible feelings (and many more) have the potential of being dominant enhancers or inhibitors in your response.

Vehicular comedy and the assumed audience

We often think of "the public" differently than we think of ourselves, our families, or any social group we happen to be in. In intimate groups of adults, we can hear the raunchiest or most racist joke, but we know it's only a joke. But if that joke goes out into the public arena, we may feel that America is getting sent the wrong message or that people won't understand that it's just a harmless joke. We may feel a sense of moral outrage over material we privately enjoy.

On the other hand, we may enjoy the subversion in a *risqué* message or material that openly pokes fun at sacred cows. The recognition of subversion can evoke joy, anger, and feelings of superiority in one receiver, while it can stir outrage in another.

Our response to vehicular comedy can be affected by other receivers even when they aren't in the same space with us. Vehicles make us assume the existence of other receivers. When we read a book, for example, we know that it has been made available to the masses and that others will read the same material.

This makes us critical of the joke's effect on our idea of the masses. We may feel moral outrage if we think it inappropriate for young people. This knowledge may temper our enjoyment of the joke, even though we're completely alone.

Aspect of awareness 5: Response comparison with other receivers

In this aspect of awareness, our response is actually affected by the responses of other receivers.

When receiving comedy in groups, we are very aware of other people's reactions. We measure ourselves against the group in a number of ways. We may bond with them through the shared experience, but we may also measure how quickly we get the jokes compared to others. ("I got it before Aunt Gladys!") Here we have the enhancer of superiority, but in regard to other receivers rather than the source or characters in the joke.

It is the nature of things that whoever holds the floor in group communication has power, simply by holding and manipulating the attention of others. Because the source holds the power, there may be a subtle jockeying for position among receivers as they vie for the source's favor or attention. This may be a motivating factor in the formation of dominant laughers. There are always going to be teacher's pets.

There is also the concept of inclusion/exclusion. We can see evidence of it when the source delivers an inside joke. This divides the audience into those who get it and those who don't—and each member knows what side he's on. The ones who get it may feel closer to the source, while feeling superior to those who are excluded from the group.

Inside jokes may either contain specialized information (e.g. a reference only plumbers would get), or information that is available to all, but not widely known by the masses. In sitcoms, we always called these jokes "10 percenters" because we knew that only 10% of the audience would get them. The response by those few people was always huge, greatly enhanced by superiority over other receivers. Their loud laughter was a social announcement that they got the joke.

Why would we feel superior if we're part of a minority? Because our minority includes the source, and the source has the power. His or her inclusion legitimizes us as being in the inferred "smart group" or "hip group." We are, obviously, a social species, and it is hard-wired within us to recognize where the power is. The in-group survives, while others are scorned and cast out.

Posted user comments—audience response with no impact

The response of other receivers can impact on our response. What about posted comments, such as those posted beneath a YouTube video?

These posted opinions are indeed responses by other receivers, but they do not impact on our immediate enjoyment of the video. Posted comments are read by receivers after their initial response to the video. A critique can always make one go back and look at something differently, but by then the receiver has or hasn't laughed.

[*Note: Do not* regard posted user comments as a true indication of viewer response. Posted comments are written and posted for the masses, turning receivers into sources. They are not visceral reactions.]

Aspects of awareness and unintentional comedy

Unintentional comedy is that which is not formally presented as humor. It stems from the receiver's reality, most often as a recognition of incongruity. With no formal presentation of a joke, there is no critiquing of the "performance." If we were going to design a separate chart for unintentional comedy, it might look like this:

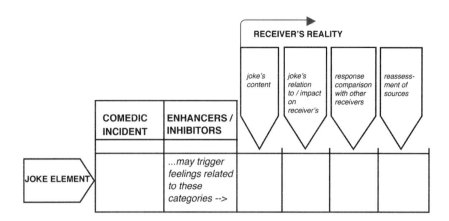

11

Elements of the joke's communication, structure, and content

11.1 RESUMING THE CHART: THE JOKE AS A WHOLE

Receivers don't tend to think of their own responses in terms of individual elements, so first we record their impression of the overall joke as it applies to the aspects of awareness:

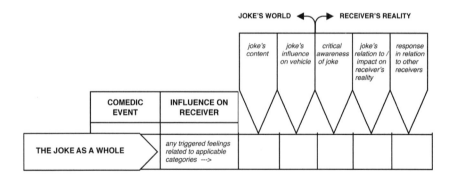

Again, it should be pointed out that a receiver may have a ton of enhancers/ inhibitors relating to one aspect and very few, even none at all, in any others.

This chart element will give us an overview of the receiver's:

- Feelings about the joke's content.

- Feelings about the joke's influence on the vehicle (if applicable). Is there appreciation of irony? Release of tension by the bringing about of a satisfying conclusion? Building of tension? Aggression? None of the above?

- Critique of the joke as a joke.

- Feelings about the joke's relation to/impact on reality. Was there external incongruity? Did the joke have an impact on the social situation? Did it build or release social tension?

- Feelings about the receiver vs. other receivers (if applicable). Did the joke make the receiver compare him- or herself to other receivers?

11.2 ELEMENTS OF COMMUNICATION AND STRUCTURE

1 Physical noise

Physical noise refers to any external stimulus that interferes with the receiver's getting the intended message. Physical noise can be as simple as static on a phone line or the noise of a plane going by or a visual distraction.

To clarify: Sometimes jokes utilize the idea of communication interference in order to create comedy, such as when a character is about to say something just as a jackhammer starts or a plane goes by and drowns him out. This is part of the joke and not physical noise as we define it—nothing has interfered with the audience's reception of the material.

In the study of communication, the larger concept of noise includes physiological noise (such as headaches) and semantic noise (involving recognition and translation of words, syntax, and referents). There is also psychological noise, which has to do with the pre-existing notions, biases, and assumptions brought into the conversation by its participants. All these types of noise have been addressed elsewhere in this model.

How physical noise can influence the receiver

Some time ago I was talking with a fan of *Frasier*, who told me she didn't much care for the previous night's episode. She immediately added, "How could anyone dress Niles in that horrible yellow shirt?" I had no recollection of this detail, and I asked her what she thought of various scenes in the episode— were they funny? She said, "I don't know, maybe ..." and got back to how much she hated the yellow shirt.

Likewise, I spent a day with a friend who had just seen *Blue Man Group*. When I asked her how it was, she responded in a disappointed tone that it wasn't that funny—and there was a woman who sat a few seats away, talking to her kid during the whole show. Three times that day we ran into people who asked her how she liked *Blue Man Group*, and each time she started off saying it wasn't good, and the first detail she went to was the woman talking to her kid.

Blue Man Group may well have been a disappointing experience. But it seems clear that there was an inhibitor at work in the constant talking of the woman a few seats away. Like Niles' yellow shirt, these sensory distractions were so powerful that they came to dominate the impression left by the experience.

The level of distraction caused by physical noise depends more on the individual receiver than on the severity of the noise itself. In the "yellow shirt" example, the visual distraction was enough to destroy the experience of comedy for one fan. Another receiver might not see it at all.

Physical noise on the chart

Physical noise is identified by the receiver. Only he or she can tell us if there were any distractions during the event:

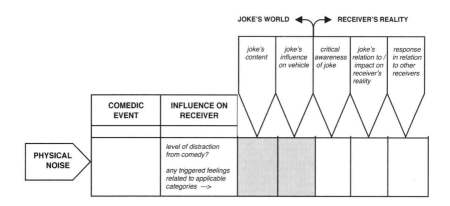

The shaded boxes denote aspects that do not apply. Physical noise cannot distract from within the world of the joke's content. Any interference will push the receiver away from the joke's reality and reinforce his or her own: that he or she is a person who is having trouble hearing or seeing a joke.

2 Basic structural features

In Part Two, we discussed various structural components of a joke, such as misleads, the rule of three, negation, container alteration, embedded punch-lines, and triggered set-ups. A basic understanding of these concepts (and others described) is enough for one to sketch out some of the more easily recognizable structural elements of any joke.

[*A gentle reminder*: Do not slide into content-based elements here. We do not want to know that it's an insult joke or a political joke or an ironic obser-vation. This is about how the information has been disseminated.]

How structural features can influence the receiver

Many receivers don't see any formal structure beneath their comedy. Others may only be aware of a feeling of familiarity triggered by the rhythm of delivery. (Jokes of similar structure can often be executed with similar delivery.) Still others are familiar with at least standard joke structures, such as the mislead.

We not only critique jokes by how funny they are, but by how they're constructed. We recognize a well-designed puzzle, and our appreciation for being tricked into creating the final picture can be enough to drive a laugh out of us.

I've known many people who particularly enjoy figuring out a joke that's a "thinker." They take pride in being the first to unlock a joke, measuring their skill against the source and other receivers.

A clever line can also make us admire the source. A Niles Crane or a Hawkeye Pierce can come up with dazzling wordplay and we like them more for it.

Familiarity

It's safe to say that whatever the joke is, the receiver has probably encountered the structure before, perhaps thousands of times. Usually, by the time the receiver starts to recognize structural elements in jokes, familiarity is already influencing his or her response.

Recognition of structural elements tends to pull focus from the joke's reality and put emphasis on the receiver's reality, where the joke is acknowledged as a joke. The content of the comedy is overwhelmed by the structure constantly announcing: "This is a joke. Now here comes the punchline."

In turn, this may have an effect on how the receiver sees the source of the joke. "Does he really think I don't see this coming?" While this may make the receiver feel superior to the source, that kind of superiority does not add to the laugh. If anything, it detracts. The source is not to be rewarded here.

Familiarity with structures may also make a receiver feel smarter than other receivers. He or she may laugh just a little ahead of everyone else just to prove he or she is ahead of the joke, nodding knowingly as the punchline finally comes rolling in. I've seen it. I'm embarrassed to say I've probably done it.

Basic structural features on the chart

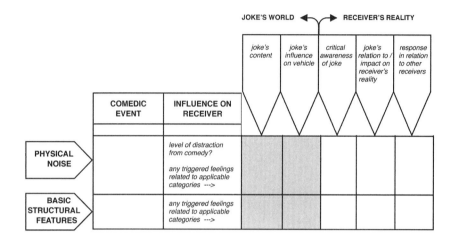

If the receiver is not always aware of structure, how can we measure his or her feelings for it? Perhaps we can find a subconscious preference, by presenting the receiver with jokes containing similar content but different structures and see if there's a pattern of cognitive preference.

3 Level of cognitive process

Here we note the cognitive process required to assemble the joke. The levels are low (SI), medium (gap-filling), and high (recontextualization).

If we were gathering data on comedy response, we would also note the level of cognitive process employed by the receiver. Remember: familiarity allows the receiver to skip steps in order to solve the joke. Therefore, a joke may require gap-filling or recontextualization in its structure, but the receiver may take them in at an SI level. This disparity is an important one to detect.

Level of cognitive process on the chart

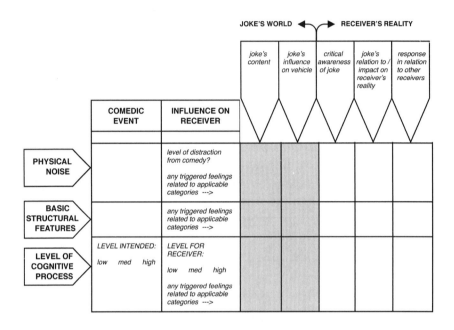

This chart asks for the intended level of cognitive process, allowing that the receiver's level may be different. If we were logging my response to "I shot an elephant in my pajamas," it would look like this:

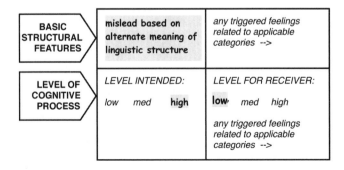

11.3 ELEMENTS OF CONTENT

1 Incongruity

Here we look at the joke's level of incongruity. As you recall, the levels are low (not unlikely), medium, (unlikely), and high (impossible).

We are also noting the type of incongruity. We did a whole section on that, remember?

Incongruity on the chart

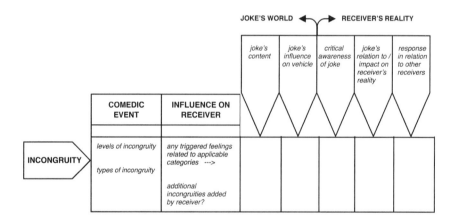

Additional incongruities added by the receiver

We know that a joke can have a ripple effect in the mind of the receiver. In visualizing the incongruous picture, he may augment the concept by supplying new incongruities.

It is extremely valuable to look for receiver-generated incongruities. We may find that a great deal of what we call sense of humor is defined by how we interact creatively with the incongruous picture.

2 Delivery

While the delivery or execution of a joke seems like an element of commu-nication rather than content, I include it here because there are times when a joke and its performance are one and the same. The silent cinema is full of examples. We may have feelings triggered by Chaplin's character in the boxing ring in *City Lights*, while we simultaneously step back and marvel at the performance of Chaplin the actor.

Thus, "delivery" refers to the performance of the material, whether linguistic or physical. It includes artistic delivery as well, as in graphic-based comedy.

How delivery can influence the receiver

How important is delivery? Certainly we've all seen someone mangle a perfectly good joke, turning it into a useless pile of words and awkward pauses. On the other end of the spectrum, I've seen comedians tell mediocre jokes and get huge laughs because their timing and inflection were impec-cable. Back in my stand-up days, I was on stage doing a callback to a joke when I realized that I'd forgotten to tell the original joke—I was now saying something that would make no sense. But I was on a roll, so I went with it anyway. Huge laugh. And I launched into the next joke before the audience could stop and think.

In this case there were strong reception factors at work. The audience had been enjoying the act thus far, and they liked me. But they'd also been lulled into my rhythms. There is an innate understanding of comedy rhythm. When we get to hearing the right kinds of words emphasized and the familiar pauses for tension, and when we see the right visual cues in manner and expression, we understand that comedy is being generated. In a way, it's like the music without the lyrics. The audience will, under the right circumstances, laugh at pure delivery.

There are many many, ways to screw up joke delivery. I knew a guy who used to be good at telling jokes. Unfortunately, someone complimented him for his storytelling abilities, and he began to draw out the jokes, embellishing them with meaningless details—he was trying to be funnier than the joke. He got to be as bad as those people who say "um" all the time and remember the joke's information all out of order.

Delivery on the chart

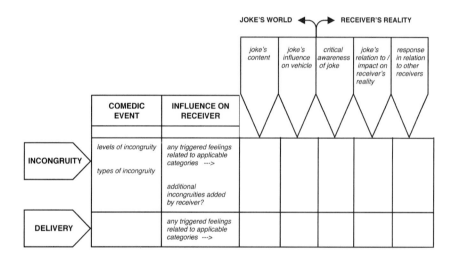

If you want to see how important delivery is, try this. The next time you hear a fantastic joke on TV, write it down, and have other people (who didn't see it) perform it. Try a number of different people. See where they pause, what they emphasize. See how the joke fares when the delivery is weak.

3 Knowledge of material origin

Where did the comedy come from? Was it written by a professional? Ad libbed? Was it simply a serendipitous occurrence?

The receiver may or may not have knowledge about the origin of the material in the joke. That knowledge—or lack of knowledge—can affect joke response.

This is one of those rare instances in which we have a chart element that's based on the individual receiver rather than being an objective part of the joke or its communication. However, I don't want to gloss over it, so in the chart it goes. Who's going to stop me?

How knowledge of material origin can influence the receiver

There are four options here:

1   *Material exists prior to event, new to receiver*: When Bob tells me the joke about the guy walking into the bar, I know that the joke predates this exchange, even though it's new to me. This is also true of any packaged comedy: films, written material, prepared monologues, etc.

2   *Material exists prior to event, familiar to receiver*: Now Bob's telling me a joke I've heard before. I may compare his execution to my prior experience with the joke, or I may be irritated if Bob tries to pass this joke off as his own.

How often have we been in a social gathering where someone tries to pass off a movie quote as an original line? Somebody always has to call him on it. I imagine that this somebody (Okay, it's me) feels pretty superior to the source.

I may be irritated with other receivers for laughing at such old material, and this may trigger superiority. I'm really a jerk. This book is opening my eyes.

I may be watching a film and see a bit I've seen in other films. My recognition of the pillaged material may take me out of the film's reality. [*Note:* If a character in a film intentionally does an old bit and that's the point of the joke—perhaps with a wink to the audience—I may feel differently, since the material is not being passed off as new.]

3   *Material generated in the moment*: This would be ad libbing, or improvised comedy. Knowing that this material is being generated on the spot will likely increase my appreciation for the source. Even if the joke itself is not stellar, I may admire the quickness with which the source came up with it. The next time you see an evening of improv, imagine how much you or the audience would be enjoying the show if you thought that the very material you were watching had actually been written and rehearsed prior to the performance. Chances are that you'd find it boring. Improv thrives on flashes of brilliance, and since audiences know this, they'll wade patiently through stretches of substandard attempts.

This is also one of the reasons why people will laugh heartily at a joke ad libbed at the dining room table but roll their eyes at the same joke in a sitcom.

4   *Material serendipitous, not packaged as comedy*: This is unintentional comedy, those serendipitous occurrences that we stumble on during the course of our lives. And because we know it's not prepared or intended as comedy, we never go in with expectations. With no expectations, some pretty mild comedy can get laughs. My dad once noticed an incongruity: in Las Vegas there's an Italian restaurant in a

French-themed casino. He thought this was hysterical. I wonder if he'd have laughed if it had appeared in a film.

ANECDOTE ALERT

Some time ago, a friend of mine was watching *The Wizard of Oz* on TV. During the twister scene, an actual tornado warning crawled across the bottom of the screen. Finding the coincidence amusing, she popped in a tape and recorded it.

Later, she was playing it for a colleague at Cleveland State University when a few students wandered into the classroom. They saw the footage but didn't find it funny. When asked why, they responded, "Because we didn't know if it was intentional or not."

The footage was later shown to different groups of students. Some were told it was a coincidence caught on tape, and others were told that it had been manufactured as a joke. The ones who thought the tape had been made as a joke actually found it *less* funny than the ones who knew it was a coincidence. This makes perfect sense: as an intentional joke it's not that funny. As a coincidence we may get extra enjoyment from knowing the odds against this combination of elements occurring simultaneously. Of course, there were some students who found it definitely not funny, because "tornadoes are never funny." In these cases, humor was overcome by negative reaction to the content.

Knowledge of material origin on the chart

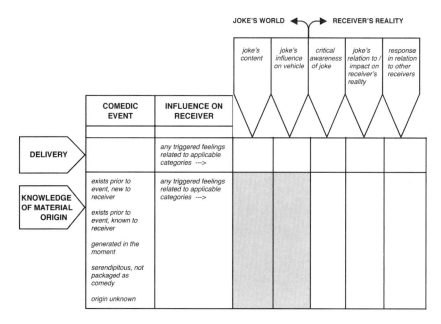

Notice that the receiver's knowledge of the material's origin only comes from aspects in the receiver's reality. Once the receiver thinks in terms of the information being "material," he is looking at the joke from outside.

There is an interesting experiment to be done here. If we could assemble a number of jokes and tell different groups of people different stories about the jokes' origins, we might see if there is any affect on the receivers' critical assessments of the material.

11.4 THE TARGET

A great deal of comedy centers on a target. This is a person or entity that is made to look or feel negative in some way through the context or use of a joke. The joke can draw attention to a flaw or misstep in the target, such as ugliness, ignorance, pomposity, greed, or any number of traits we'd like to minimize as part of our own personal make-up.

The source can be the target, as in self-deprecating humor. The receiver can also be the target, or it can be a third entity.

How the target can influence the receiver

A receiver's pre-joke feelings for a target will enhance or inhibit his response to the joke.

Here's an old joke:

> Two Polish hunters have killed a deer and are struggling to drag it head-first to their truck, when a passerby offers them a suggestion. "You know, if you drag that deer the other way, it'll be easier—the antlers won't dig into the ground." After he leaves, they decide to try it. After ten minutes, one says, "This is easier all right." And the other one says, "Yeah, but we're getting farther from the truck."

Polish people are pretty much the target here, although they, like your mama, are generally considered placeholder joke people. Even so, there are some politically correct receivers who will be offended. In Texas, the same joke might be reconfigured so that the target is Oklahomans. I originally heard it about George W. Bush and his father. Feelings about Bush were very volatile—the joke got huge laughs from Democrats and not much of a response from Republicans, except maybe anger.

A receiver need not have pre-joke feelings for the target in order to be affected by the target's role in the joke. A random audience member may be ridiculed by a comedian. While we have no personal connection with this target, it's possible that our empathy will cause us to vicariously feel the shame and embarrassment of being publicly singled out. We may also revel in the sadistic torture of this person. In this case, we identify with both the source and the receiver.

The actor behind the character

A receiver's feelings for the target in a narrative performance will be influenced by his or her feelings for the actor playing the role. Something to be aware of.

Triggered feelings about the target

Here's where identification comes in big time.

Imagine you are in a comedy club and a comic insults one of the other audience members. Putting aside the actual content of the joke, here are some of the ways in which identification can affect your experience of the event:

Identification with source …	*Identification with target …*
can bring up vicarious feelings of	can bring up vicarious feelings of

- anger
- enjoyment of control
- superiority over target

- shame
- embarrassment
- fear
- enjoyment of attention

This is not even a full list of the possibilities. Aside from all the identifying, you may be experiencing any of the following:

- envy of the target's attention
- relief at not being the target
- feelings of aggression toward the target
- your own superiority over the target
- inclusion with other receivers
- inclusion with the source

- disapproval of the source's actions

- admiration for the source

Some of these feelings can enhance the experience, some can inhibit.

We often feel that the role of target must be earned. In vehicular comedy, as in life, we enjoy seeing a character with negative traits—cruelty, arrogance, etc.—being knocked down a peg. Triumph over evil, or at least pretension, can make a good joke applause-worthy.

The target on the chart

In this chart, the column on the left provides for more specific identification of the target, as well as the target's relationship to the receiver and the target in relation to the joke.

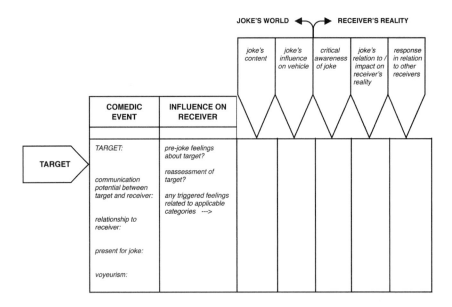

Target

Here we identify the target or target group. Be aware of the difference between a character and the actor playing the character. In *Road to Utopia*, Duke (Bing Crosby) may take a shot at Chester (Bob Hope), making Chester the target. On the other hand, when Crosby steps out of character to take a shot at Bob Hope, Hope is the target.

Communication potential between target and receiver

Does the receiver have the ability to communicate with the target or any representative of the targeted group during the joke, through laughter, speech, or other behavior? One might laugh all day at racist humor, but be just a little less enthusiastic when an actual African American/Mexican/Asian is in the vicinity.

This goes back to those people who were in the room when Stephen Colbert raked George W. Bush over the coals in a monologue performed with the target in the room. Their potential for communication with the target almost certainly tempered the response.

Relationship to receiver

This could run the gamut. It could be none, self, employee of target, married to target, etc. If you are of Polish descent hearing a Polack joke, your relationship would be group affiliation.

Here's a good one: my mom collects Slovenian jokes. Why? Because she's married to a Slovenian. When she hears or reads a joke in which the target is "a Slovenian," her relationship to the target is marriage to a representative of the target group. This relationship brings a delightful level of passive aggressiveness to her thrill at the finding and sticking-on-the-refrigerator of these jokes.

Let's limit this category to personal relationships or group affiliation. If the joke is about the president and you have no actual connection to him besides being a citizen of the United States, you may have strong feelings about him, but you have no relationship with him.

Present for jokes

A target can be present for the jokes, as George Bush was at the aforementioned correspondents' dinner. His presence affects our response to the jokes—see how much more tension there is than if someone just makes a crack about the president on a TV show? If Moe slaps Curly, Curly is present for the joke, even if he's not aware that it's a joke.

Voyeurism

Sometimes the target is present for—but not privy to—the very jokes they're a part of. This takes us into the area of the practical joke and voyeurism. Voyeurism can only occur when the target is a real life being as opposed to a fictional one. A fictional character may not be aware that he's in a joke, but his "unawareness" is not real, it's only part of the dramatic conceit.

Voyeurism is a staple of vehicular comedy, from the early days of *Candid Camera* to 2006's *Borat: Cultural Learnings of America for Make Benefit Glorious Nation of Kazakhstan*. A great deal of our enjoyment comes from the knowledge that the targets are not aware that they're part of a joke. (If we thought the targets were in on the jokes, would the comedy be nearly as entertaining?)

Homework for the hardcore comedy detective

Practice identifying comedic targets:

1   *Target #1.* In a Three Stooges short, Moe twists Curly's nose with
    pliers.

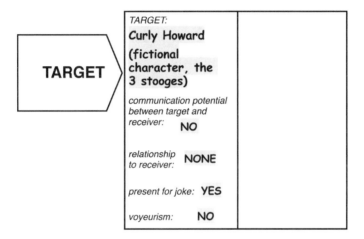

Note that the targeted Curly is actually a fictional construct, played by
an actor who went by that stage name.

2   *Target #2.* A comedian tells a joke in which "a black guy" is the butt of
    the joke. The audience is racially mixed and the receiver is black.

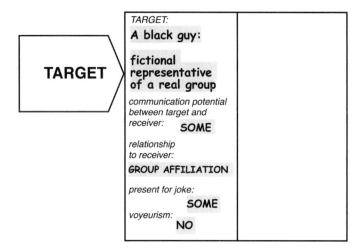

Again, although the target is a fictional construct, he is generically identified by group affiliation, which makes "blacks" the actual target. Note here the use of "some." Clearly the entire target group cannot be present, but there are others present who represent the group.

3   *Target #3.* In the previous scenario only the receiver is white. Will the presence of black audience members affect his response.

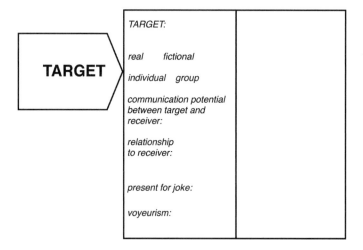

4 *Target #4.* You look out of your office window and laugh when you see a man across the street fall into a puddle. (PS: You can be a real jerk sometimes.)

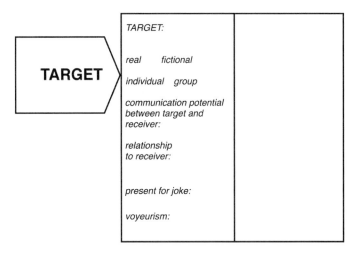

5 *Target #5.* You're at a comedy club and the woman on stage is the mother of a stranger in the audience. She makes a joke about how lame he is.

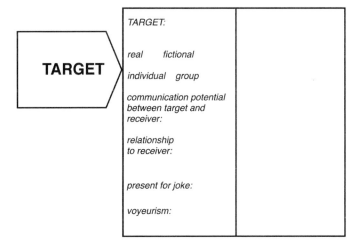

Did I trick you on that one?

5 Other elements of content

Finally, we account for the uniqueness of individual jokes. Since we can't possibly list every element of content for every joke in the world, we simply create space to allow for any specific elements that may affect receiver response.

This is a catch-all category, where one might cite the level of violence in a joke, or the use of crazy sound effects, or any other element that is specific to the individual joke.

Random words, no matter how innocent, can unexpectedly trigger feelings in a receiver. Years ago there was a popular comedy sketch called *Niagara Falls* (or *Slowly I Turn*), in which a character is triggered into an insane rage whenever he hears the words "Niagara Falls." You just never know what's going to trigger people.

Other elements of content on the chart

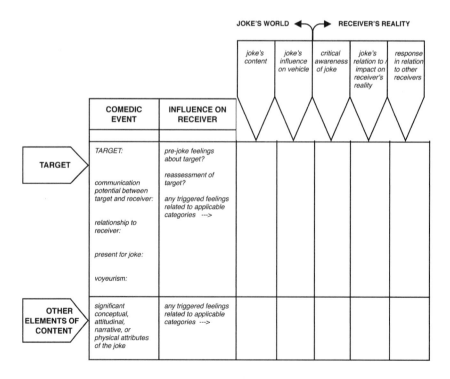

SUMMING IT ALL UP

THE COMPLETED CHART

At this point, each section of the model has been mapped in detail and all the major comedic variables have been discussed. And so, young comedy detective, you have the tools you need to understand the laugh.

If you grasp the concepts in this book, you don't need to walk around with a chart, trying to scribble down every variable of every comedic event you see. By now you should be able to witness or engage in a comedic interaction and sense which variables are likely to be dominant response factors. The more you do it, the more you will understand and appreciate the true language of laughter.

Before we call it a night, let's take a look at the chart we've built and see all the variables that may come into play for any comedic event.

Chart section 1

	ELEMENTS OF COMEDIC EVENT	**INFLUENCE ON RECEIVER**
RECEIVER PROFILE	*baseline reception factors* *physical state* *preexisting mood*	
ADDITIONAL RECEIVER ROLES		
LEVEL OF SOCIAL INTERACTION	*communication potential with other receivers:* *communication potential with source:*	
MODE OF COMMUNICATION		
DEVICE	*type:* *specific:*	

Chart section 2

	VEHICULAR COMEDY	
OUTER VEHICLES	*type:* *specific:*	
IMMEDIATE VEHICLE	*type:* *specific:*	
DIRECTION OF COMMUNICATION	*direct* *hybrid* *indirect*	**RECEIVER ROLE:** *active* *passive* *dual*
VICARIOUS COMMUNICATION WITH OTHER RECEIVERS	*none* *high* *low*	

Chart section 3

	ELEMENTS OF COMEDIC EVENT	INFLUENCE ON RECEIVER
LEVEL OF CONTROL	*low* *medium* *high*	
SOURCE	*primary source:* *relationship to receiver:*	
CONTRIBUTING SOURCES	*contributing sources and their relationship to the receiver:*	

Incongruity

Note levels and types of incongruity, multiple incongruities, look for receiver augmented incongruities.

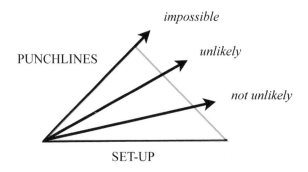

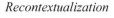

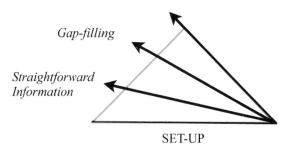

Cognitive process

Note the level of cognitive process required for the receiver to understand the comedic information. Also look for basic joke structures, such as misleads, altered containers, the rule of three, embedded punchlines, and triggered set-ups.

Enhancers/Inhibitors

Chart section 4: The joke as a whole

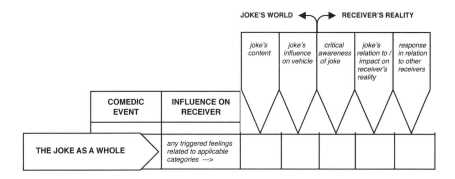

Chart section 5: Elements of communication and structure

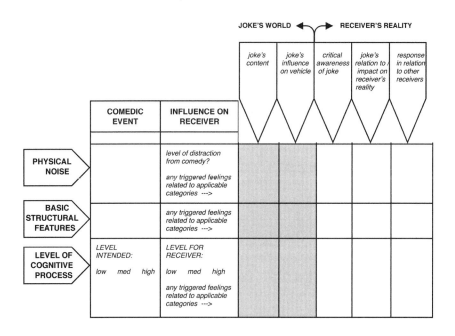

Chart section 6: Elements of content

JOKE'S WORLD ◄——————► RECEIVER'S REALITY

	COMEDIC EVENT	INFLUENCE ON RECEIVER	joke's content	joke's influence on vehicle	critical awareness of joke	joke's relation to / impact on receiver's reality	response in relation to other receivers
INCONGRUITY	levels of incongruity types of incongruity	any triggered feelings related to applicable categories ---> additional incongruities added by receiver?					
DELIVERY		any triggered feelings related to applicable categories --->					
KNOWLEDGE OF MATERIAL ORIGIN	exists prior to event, new to receiver exists prior to event, known to receiver generated in the moment serendipitous, not packaged as comedy origin unknown	any triggered feelings related to applicable categories --->					
TARGET	TARGET: communication potential between target and receiver: relationship to receiver: present for joke: voyeurism:	pre-joke feelings about target? reassessment of target? any triggered feelings related to applicable categories --->					
OTHER ELEMENTS OF CONTENT	significant conceptual, attitudinal, narrative, or physical attributes of the joke	any triggered feelings related to applicable categories --->					

Final thoughts and acknowledgments

Recently, more than a few people have asked me if writing this book has affected the way I write comedy. Do I think about triangles and enhancers and inhibitors while I'm constructing jokes? The answer is a little difficult to describe, but here goes.

The part of my brain that writes comedy doesn't seem to formally know or care about most of the information in this book. I certainly don't start off by thinking of jokes in terms of triangles. It's as though my creative side writes the comedy almost instinctively, often based on what I find amusing. Then the analytical side goes back and retraces my steps to see how I did it. That side of me also watches other people write, watches people laugh, while comparing and contrasting jokes and responses. While I can now point at a joke and quickly understand what its strengths are in relation to the model in this book (like a low incongruity joke that contains strong emotional enhancers), the formal analysis doesn't enter my conscious mind until after the writing is done.

The other question I get asked is this: "Doesn't analyzing take the fun out of comedy?"

I understand the idea behind the question. If we've reduced all comedy to a book of variables and patterns, have we taken away the magic? I believe the opposite is true. For within those patterns and variables are endless comedic possibilities. Instead of thinking of comedy in terms of jokes, I now think in terms of experiences. In doing so, the true scope of comedy is revealed. Every joke can have a million lives, be experienced a million ways. The magic is in the process and I am awed by it. I expect that I will continue to be.

* * *

The leap from studying comedy to writing a book about it was an enormous one for me, and it would not have happened—could not have happened—had

I not met two extraordinary instructors in the Communications Department at Cleveland State University.

Dr. Jack Powers (who wasn't a doctor then) was responsible for bringing me to CSU to talk about sitcom writing with his students. He introduced me to Dr. Kim Neuendorf, who has a passionate interest in the study of comedy. She shared with me some testing she had done on individual senses of humor, which I found fascinating. We had long discussions about comedy and comedic preferences.

As we talked, I kept bumping up against the idea that comedy response testing must be limited because there was not a solid comedy model in place; there was no Unified Field Theory, as it were. And in the back of my mind I began to wonder how I would approach the idea. I wasn't serious about it—I thought of it the way one might take a few minutes and try to solve perpetual motion.

What I ended up showing to Kim and Jack was a very rudimentary progression of the sequence in this book: reception factors, the triangle, and enhancers/inhibitors. At the time, the triangle was a mere construct of set-up, punchline, and "assumed knowledge." "Cognitive process"—one of the many terms coined by Kim, like "brief cognitive thrill" and "core variables"—hadn't been defined yet.

I would have probably wandered away from the whole thing early on, but Kim kept experimenting with the triangle, assigning different properties to the sides, changing angles. What would happen to the process if this angle were fixed or if we extended this line? I have many emails where we sent pictures of triangles back and forth between Cleveland and Los Angeles. She kept pushing for more flexibility (which we eventually got) and I fixed the bottom angles at 45 degrees and came up with methods of quantification. It started coming together.

Meanwhile, Jack moved away to teach at Ithaca, but whenever I could make it to Cleveland, he would drive into town just to spend a few hours talking over the latest version of the triangle with Kim and me in a commandeered classroom at Cleveland State. Jack is the one who proposed how the set-up causes us to refer to our ever-existing mental "library of normative behavior."

We discussed, we argued, and I'd scribble new diagrams on the boards. For a short while, there was actually a two-triangle model!

Throughout the process, Jack and Kim would not only come up with ideas, but ask questions that would reveal flaws in my thinking. (They were truly the kid in the back.) One time I met Jack in Las Vegas and he asked me a simple question that made me throw out nearly half of the book. That was not a good day.

As the project kept growing, the two of them read every draft, making extensive notes. Jack liked the writing to be more conversational, and Kim honed in on a phrase that I used one time in the middle of the book and suggested I make it a theme. So whenever you see the words "comedy detective" it's largely due to her.

I am not always easy to work with. I can reflexively push away new ideas when they don't fit easily into my thinking, only to realize later that the idea was exactly right. (I remember doing this with Kim when she started talking about multiple levels of incongruity.)

To Kim and Jack, I say thank you for helping, encouraging, putting up with, and challenging me. Thank you for taking the time out of your lives to explore this with me. Your intellect and friendship is valued.

There were others who helped along the way, like Dr. Patty Burant, also from CSU, who told me about superiority being an ongoing social need. Dr. Graeme Ritchie, from the University of Aberdeen, was invaluable in showing me where I could clarify some ideas and even how to structure the chapters. Then there are those friends who took the time to slog through early drafts, like Terry Hughes and Dennis Palumbo and Mai Nguyen, and Pat and Laurel Sullivan. Many of these people had to listen to me whining during the times of self-doubt and they never stopped encouraging me.

Also, a shout out to Tom Anderson, Jim Kraizel, Jeff Swiney. We started out in stand-up together and spent innumerable nights at Denny's trying to top each other, taking our first rudimentary steps in comedy experimentation. Tom and I went on to write for *Cheers*, and he still makes me laugh as hard as I did when I was 19.

And there's Phil Skerry, from Lakeland Community College, who sent me to Continuum and the able guidance of Katie Gallof. And Anne King and Kim Storry, who skilfully turned a pile of words and shapes into an actual book. Thank you so much!

And finally, there is one other person to whom this book owes its existence, and that is my wife, Daphne Pollon. Not only has she had to deal with my mind wandering 24 hours a day—imagine trying to have dinner with me while I mentally turn everything you say into a triangle—but she also volunteered to run our lives so that I could hole myself up in an apartment for months at a time to write. Without that gift, I'd never have finished. Being a writer herself, she also had great notes, primarily: simpler, simpler, simpler. She was right. Thank you, Daphne. I owe you about four hundred triangle-free dinners.

INDEX

Abbott and Costello 110
ad libbing 271
Adams, Douglas 98
Addams, Charles 139, 181
Addams Family, The 82, 169
aggression 2
Alda, Alan 190
Alfie 86
Allen, Woody 146, 156, 159, 231
alliteration 171
alternate interpretations 194–5
Amazing Spider-Man, The 88
America's Funniest Home Videos 71
Andy Griffith Show, The 15, 82, 206
announcement 60
applause 37
appreciation 119, 204, 206, 209
Arthur 189
Arthur, Bea 221
assumed audience 256
At the Circus 129, 196
audience 37, 61, 62, 78, 81, 82, 83
    response 258
    studio audience 69, 80
audio 45
Avery, Tex 152
awareness 12–13, 14, 247–59

Ball, Lucille 100
belly-laugh 203–5
Beverly Hillbillies, The 82
Big 148
Billy Madison 149
Birds, The 214, 215
bloopers 57–8, 152
Blue Man Group 262
Blues Busters 194

bodily function humor 206, 222
bonding 36
Borat 278
Brooks, Albert 232
Brooks, Mel 171, 204, 214, 255
Bruce, Lenny 231
Bugs Bunny 227
Burns, George 94
Bush, George W. 252, 277, 278

Caesar, Sid 147
callbacks 219–20, 268
Calvin and Hobbes 1
Candid Camera 278
canned laughter 82
Carlin, George 125, 164, 165, 183
cartoons 98, 139, 181
Cavett, Dick 26
Chaplin, Charlie 47, 158, 198, 268
Cheers 58, 65–6, 94, 192, 196, 197, 216,
    227
City Lights 158, 268
cognitive development 29
cognitive process 111, 114–15, 117, 118,
    119, 120, 179, 186, 202–5, 206, 209,
    229–31, 235, 286
    angles 116–17
    levels 156–8, 161–3, 179, 196, 265–6
cognitive requirements 155–6
coincidence 4, 272
Colbert Report, The 176
Colbert, Stephen 176–7, 252, 277
combination modes 45–6
comedic entropy 127
comedic event 7–16, 37
    documenting 16–19
comedic idea 115

comedic information 7, 11, 16, 18, 49, 108
comedic potential 25–7
    triggers 25–7
comedy
    misfires 112
    politically oriented 231
    response 230
    rhythm 268
    socially oriented 231
    theories 1–7
Comedy Central Roast 197
communication 37, 38
    direction of 78–9
    modes 43–9
    potential 42
    vicarious 80–4
containers 171–6
    altered 174, 286
    linguistic 171–3
    triggered 215
    visual 175
content 282
content providers 63–4
context 55
    narrative 55
Cosby, Bill 98, 102, 103, 119, 206, 239
Crosby, Bing 277
cruelty 2
Curb Your Enthusiasm 69–70

Daily Show, The 75, 219
Dangerfield, Rodney 227
Dead Men Don't Wear Plaid 233
decoding 46–7
delayed takes 220
delivery 26, 254, 268–9
    rhythm 264
devices 49–54
disappointment 5
    theory 5
Diva 154
double entendre 185, 199
double meanings 193–4, 229

double takes 220
dramatic context 223, 227, 251
Duck Soup 149
Dunham, Jeff 102

Ellen 83–4
emoticons 27, 29–32
emotional enhancers 29
emotional responses 146
emotions 241, 242
    amplifiers 246–7
    manipulation 240
    triggered 250–1
empathy 148, 274
Enchanted 166
enhancers 12–13, 14, 16, 25, 206, 208, 222, 239–41, 243, 244, 256, 257, 260, 287–8
entropy 222–35
exclusion 247
expectations 64, 66–8
    creating 168–71
    thwarting 167–8

Facebook 62
    posts 62–3
familiarity 264–5
Far Side, The 99
feelings, triggered 275–6
Ferris Bueller's Day Off 78
"found" humor 27
Four Seasons, The 190
fourth wall 78
Foxx, Redd 232
Frasier 72, 83, 152–3, 159, 240, 251, 262
Freud, Sigmund 3

gap-filling 181–2, 184, 186, 195, 196, 230, 265
gatekeeping 66
Gelbart, Larry 204
Get Smart 82
Gilligan's Island 82
Gold Rush, The 47
Golden Girls, The 221

Gorcey, Leo 194
Gould, Howard 154
Grammer, Kelsey 94, 153
Green Acres 82
group affiliation 277, 280
group identity 37
Gulliver's Travels 215

Hall, Huntz 194
Hanks, Tom 148
Hardy, Oliver 78, 151, 222
head-laugh 203–5
Heisenberg, Werner 35
Henry, O. 5
High Anxiety 214
His Girl Friday 1
Hitchcock, Alfred 214
Hitchhiker's Guide to the Galaxy, The 98
Honeymooners, The 246
Hope, Bob 140, 277
humor
    self-deprecating 274
    sick 232
Hunt, Bonnie 69–70
hype 67–8
hyperbole 154

I Love Lucy 56, 70, 97, 100, 158
identification 3, 119, 206, 245–7
Idle Class, The 198
impossibilities 143
improvisation 69–70, 90, 99, 271
inappropriateness 151
inclusion 247
incongruity 5, 11, 13, 15, 25, 28, 31, 108–9,
        114–15, 117, 118, 119, 120, 156,
        174–5, 177–8, 197, 202–5, 206, 210,
        212, 215, 217, 218, 220, 221, 223, 225,
        226–9, 233, 239, 244, 258, 267, 286
    angles 115–16, 214
    of association 154
    attitudinal 146–7
    behavioral 147–9
    conceptual 145–6

creating 124–5
definition 121
dominant 128–9, 212
intent incongruity 153
levels 134, 135–6, 137, 140, 142, 267
logical 153
multiple 128, 210, 211–16
personal 150–1
physical 151–2
qualifying 133
reception incongruity 153
relative 127–8
safe 202
secondary 128–9, 212
types 145–54
incongruity resolution 12, 130–2
    theory 115
incongruous image 181
inhibitors 12–13, 14, 16, 25, 29, 208,
        240–1, 256, 260, 287–8
inside jokes 257
interactivity 62, 90
internal logic 109
ironic comedy 57–8
irony 4–5, 225

Jack Benny Program 181
Jerk, The 220
jokes 23, 24
    content 249–51
    definition 18–19
    inside 257
    "knock-knock" jokes 199–201
    one-line 183
    self-contained 227
    stand-alone 98–9
    structures 286
joke-type 23

Kaufman, Andy 233–4
Kaufman, George S. 172, 173, 174
Keaton, Buster 148, 150, 158
Kid Brother, The 167
King of the Hill 163

King, Stephen 57
"knock-knock" jokes 199–201
knowledge
    assumed 177–80
    planted 180–1

LA Times 74
Larsen, Gary 99
laughter 19, 25, 27–32, 35, 82, 83
    canned 82
laugh-track 80, 82
Laurel, Stan 151, 222
Leachman, Cloris 197
Lehrer, Tom 85
Lemmon, Jack 149
Letterman, David 83
Lewis, Jerry 168
linguistic structures 194
live comedy 30, 61
live performance 37, 46
Lloyd, David 109
Lloyd, Harold 158, 167, 168
LOL 37
Lucky Ducky 152

M*A*S*H* 82, 179
Mad 64, 232
Mad Libs 90, 121
Martin, Dean 168
Martin, Demetri 46
Martin, Steve 220, 225, 232–3
Marx Brothers 129
Marx, Groucho 114, 148–9
Mary Tyler Moore Show, The 58
material origin 270–3
Matrix, The 234
meta-comedy 121–2
Miller, George 195
Minsky, Marvin 24
misinterpretation 192, 229
misleads 192, 229, 286
Mr. Ed 82, 127, 129
Modern Family 98, 101
Mona Lisa (painting) 175

Monkees, The 82
monologues 59, 78, 97, 239
Monty Python's Flying Circus 5, 15, 68
multiple receivers 39, 255
Munsters, The 82
Murphy, Eddie 78
My Three Sons 82

negation 187–9
Niagara Falls 282
Nielson, Leslie 188
Night at the Opera, A 129
non-vehicular comedy 56–9, 95
non-vehicular response 57–8
nostalgia 119, 206

observational comedy 182–3
Office, The 68–9
one-line joke 183
ongoing comedy 227–8
Onion, The 150

paradox 24, 26
Parker, Dorothy 178–9
parody 214–16, 234, 235
    definition 214
pattern recognition 23
Patty Duke Show, The 82
performance 44–5, 46, 59
physical noise 261–3
physical state 33
physiological noise 262
play on words see wordplay
portable comedy 235
practical jokes 209–10
problem solving 230
Producers, The 171
pulp fiction 4
punchline 93, 95, 102, 110, 111, 113, 117,
        122, 123, 124, 130, 131, 133, 135,
        141, 144, 153, 164, 165, 168, 170,
        174, 181, 184, 185, 190, 191, 192,
        194, 201, 217, 218, 219, 220, 229,
        243, 264, 265, 286

embedded 183–4
puns 185, 199

reaction shots 220–1
Reader's Digest 72
receiver 25, 32, 46–7, 49, 51, 56, 60–2, 71, 72, 81–4, 90, 155, 164, 167, 168–71, 174, 180, 182–4, 192, 193, 195, 209, 210, 212, 214, 218, 223, 227, 233–4, 249, 253, 262, 264, 266, 267, 268–9, 270, 271, 273, 274–6, 277–8, 279, 280
receiver response 207, 282
receiver roles 34
reception factors 10, 14, 16, 32–4
    vehicle-based 77–88
reciprocal exchange 39
recontextualization 157, 167, 168, 184–201, 229, 230, 265
relief 3–4
repetition 216–19, 226, 227, 230
response 15, 19, 28–9, 30, 36, 56, 270
response comparison 257–8
response factors 239–40, 283
rhythm 268
riddles 199–201
ridicule 243
ripple effect 267
Road to Utopia 140, 227, 277
Rocky 244
ROFLMAO 37
Ross, Jeffrey 197
"rule of three" 169, 181, 193–4

Safety Last 158, 168
sarcasm 189
satire 214–16
    definition 214
Saturday Night Live 56, 63, 77, 80, 182, 234, 248
Scarecrow, The 148
Schopenhauer, Arthur 15–16
Schulz, Charles 97
Seinfeld 159

Seinfeld, Jerry 97
self-contained jokes 227
self-contradiction 189
self-deprecating humor 274
sense of humor 224–5, 267
sensory reconstruction 47
set-up 122, 123, 131, 133, 138–9, 156, 164, 165, 167, 170, 174, 180–1, 185, 189–90, 191, 192, 195, 201, 215, 217, 218, 219, 233
    triggered 111–12, 173–4, 286
shared experience 36
shock 12
shock value 206
SI 163–6, 167, 168, 184, 186–90, 194, 196, 200, 201, 235, 239, 266
SI humor 159
sick humor 232
sitcoms 65, 68–9, 252, 257
    multi-camera 229
    single-camera 68, 70
slow burns 220
Slowly I Turn 282
smiley faces *see* emoticons
Snoopy 98
social interaction 40
    levels 35–40
social norms 148
Some Like it Hot 149
soundtracks 151
Soup, The 219
Space Jam 148
specific devices 49–54
    definition 50–1
specific vehicles 70–1, 72
spit takes 220
stage shows 76
stand-up 79
Steamboat Bill, Jr. 150, 158
still image 44
structural features 263–5
studio audience 69, 80
subversion 3
Super Hero Movie 188

superiority 3, 11–12, 241, 242–5, 251, 257,
    264, 271
surprise 167–8
Swift, Jonathan 215

takes 220–1
targets 242–3, 247, 256, 273–81
Taxi 233
tellers 97–8
tension 251
    building 166–7
text conversations 37
Three Stooges, The 1, 129, 224, 244
Three's Company 72
timing 268
Tom Sawyer 73, 76, 87
    stage production 76
Top Secret 188
Trading Places 78
tragedy 26, 244–5
transmission 124
Twain, Mark 1, 87
tweets 62–3
Twitter 62
typos 142

unexpected appropriateness 151
unintentional comedy 57–8, 258

vehicle-based reception factors 77–88

vehicles 55–77, 78
    language 65, 69–70
vehicular audiences 253
vehicular comedy 56–9, 97–9, 251–3, 254,
    256, 276
vehicular intent 57–8
vicarious communication 80–4
video *see also* YouTube 44, 46, 79
video games 90
violence 206
visual comedy 188–9
visual humor 129, 181–2
visual input 155
visual misleads 198–9
visual references 162
voyeurism 78, 278

websites 62, 90
Welch, Raquel 182
White, Betty 221
Who Wants to be a Millionaire? 243
Wilder, Gene 255
Williams, Robin 162
Wizard of Oz, The 272
wordplay 31, 95, 120, 121, 171–6, 199
written word 44, 79

Young Frankenstein 254
YouTube *see also* video 61, 63, 66, 71, 90,
    234, 243